PROBLEMS AND PROSPECTS OF RETAIL MARKETING

PROBLEMS AND PROSPECTS OF RETAIL MARKETING

Edited by

Sudhansu Sekhar Nayak

Sr. Lecturer (Commerce), R.N. College

Dura, Berhampur (Orissa)

Rajib Lochan Panigrahy

Faculty (MBA)

Ambedkar College of Management & Technology

Berhampur (Orissa)

&

Anil Kumar Sahu

Professor (MBA)

Department of Business Administration

Berhampur University (Orissa)

DISCOVERY PUBLISHING HOUSE PVT. LTD.

NEW DELHI-110 002

Published by:
Tilak Wasan

DISCOVERY PUBLISHING HOUSE PVT. LTD.
4831/24, Prahlad Street, Ansari Road
Darya Ganj, New Delhi-110002 (India)
Phone: +91-11-23279245, 43764432
Fax : +91-11-23253475
E-mail : parul.wasan@gmail.com
discoverypublishinghouse@gmail.com
info@discoverypublishinggroup.com
web : www.discoverypublishinggroup.com

***First Edition:* 2011**
ISBN: 978-81-8356-915-6

Problems and Prospects of Retail Marketing

Printed at:
Shree Balaji Art Press
Delhi

Preface

Retailing, one among the largest sectors in the global economy, is going through a transition phase not only in India but over the world. It accounts for 10 per cent of the country's GDP and 8 per cent of employment. The service sector accounts for a large share of GDP in most developed economies. And the retail sector forms a very strong component of the service sector. In short, as long as people need to buy, retailing generates employment. Globally, retailing is customer centric, with an emphasis on innovation in products, processes and services.

The network of retailers reaches every nook and corner of the country. Any product produced any where in the country can easily come to the hands of the buyers from any location due to retailing. After globalization, retail business occupies a lion's share in marketing. Now it diverts the attention not only for the Government, but also for research scholars, planners, manufacturers, economists and others in the present scenario.

S.S. Nayak
R.L. Panigrahy
A.K. Sahu

Contents

List of Contributors

1. **Dr. B. Eswar Rao Patnaik,** Reader in Economics (Retd.), S.B.R.G. Women's College, Berhampur, Ganjam, (Orissa).
2. **Dr. Sudhansu Sekhar Nayak,** Senior Faculty, Deptt. of Commerce, R.N. College, Dura, Berhampur - 10, Ganjam, (Orissa).
3. **Dr. Anil Kumar Sahu,** Professor in MBA, Berhampur University, Bhanja Bihar, Berhampur, (Orissa).
4. **Prabin Kumar Padhy,** Head, Deptt of Management, Gayatri Institute of Science and Technology, Berhampur. (Orissa).
5. **Nilima Das,** Lecturer in Marketing, Trident Academy of Creative Technology, Bhubaneswar, Orissa.
6. **Dr. Sudhakar Patra,** Reader in Economics, Ravenshaw University, Cuttack, (Orissa).
7. **Dr. Kabita Kumari Sahu,** Lecturer in Economics, North Orissa University, Baripada, (Orissa).
8. **Dr. Dibyasingh Gochhayat,** Reader in Commerce, Government Autonomous College, Phulbani.
9. **S.S. Nayak,** Lecturer in Commerce, R.N. College, Dura, Berhampur, Ganjam, (Orissa).

10. **Dr. R.Srinivasan,** Associate Professor, PG & Research Department of Corporate Secretaryship, Bharatidarshan Government College for Women (Autonomous), Puduchery.

11. **Prof (Dr.) Samarendra Mahapatra,** IMIS, Bhubaneswar, (Orissa).

12. **Rajib Lochan Panigrahy,** Faculty (MBA), Ambedkar College of Management and Technology, Berhampur, (Orissa).

13. **Dr. Achintya Mahapatra,** Sr. Lecturer, Department of Business Studies, Royal University of Bhutan, (G.C.B.S), (Bhutan).

14. **Umesh Namdev Jadhav,** Senior Lecturer, Department of Business Studies, Royal University of Bhutan, (G.C.B.S), Bhutan.

15. **Mrs. Madhusmita Das,** Faculty (Management Studies), Vignan Institute of Management andTechnology, Berhampur, Orissa.

1

Rural Retailing in India
An Overview

B. Eswar Rao Patnaik*

INTRODUCTION

A major initiative in the consumer finance is retail trade. The other forms of business verticals are capital, brands media, space and logistics. The most exciting opportunity today is at the periphery of retailing business, because being retail puts us in a unique position to attract and directly reach our million. Who reach our stores. The retail industry is the second largest provider of employment after agriculture in India. The retail industry occupies a major area in the map of development in India, by contributing 10 per cent of GDP and roughly 40 million people (8% of total work force) ore employed in the retail industry. India with over 15 million retail outlets, has the highest retail density in the world, over 95 per cent of India's retail activity is in the unorganized

* Reader in Economics (Retd.), S.B.R.G. Women's College, Berhampur, Ganjam, Orissa.

sector. Retailing in India owes its origin to the neighbourhood *kirana* stores which looked after the comforts and conveniences of the consumers.

The pendulum of the economy oscillated from manufactures to retailers, e.g food world, Planet M and music world, *subhiksha* and Nilgiri in food and FMCG in the 1990s. The ascendancy of sopping complexes is noted in urban centres in the recent past, with facilities for parking cars. The flower to the garland of retail industry in India is the accelerating development of super and hyper markets which have blessed the customers with 3Vs value, volume and variety.

RURAL RETAILING IN INDIA

Roughly 73 per cent of Indians dwell in rural areas. Kishore Biyani observes that "there are 720 million consumers who live in 62,700 villages". There are 720 million consumers who live in villages that are separated by large distance and are thinly populated. seventeen per cent of villages account for 60 per cent of rural wealth. The number of customers that a single rural outlet can attract in India is low and makes modern rural formats unviable. Rural Indians have to travel long distance to source product he seeks/sells. Thus, the wholesaler, farmer, agriproducers, retailers and consumers are disadvantageous parties. Scope exists for increasing efficiency and building a transparent price discovery mechanism.

TASK OF A RETAILER

The key to success in retailing is getting customers to your store again and again. A retailer has to create aspiration and the desire to the consumer by exposing brands to the consumer. They need brands as device to articulate their aspirations. A brand is an idea and limited brand vocabulary can not fire imagination of consumers. Retailing is the final phase of the distribution channel and hence the retailer has to ensure sufficient supplies of consumers good in the market. Though out retail business we sell every thing food, grocery, apparel, foot wear, furniture, electronics, home products, music, medicine and communication products. It follows that, the retailer has to perform the herculean task of assessing fast changing tastes of consumers and adjust the supply of consumers goods and services. There are multiple delivery channels like, hyper markets, supermarkets malls and special stores in the country. To attract a mass base, with Big Bazars the retailers may have to attract flow of borrowed funds from money market and capital market.

The onerous task of the retailer is to recognize the felt needs of the consumers. As Kishore Biyani observes we have to work closely with every developer and with whom we are engaged. We share our own knowledge, customers understanding and consumers insights.

RURAL MARKETS FEATURES OF INDIAN

1. **Large and scattered:** The typical feature of Indian villages are they are spread over 3.2 million sq. km; near by 72% of Indians live in rural areas.
2. **Lanentaby low levels of Living**: A vast segment of population in India live below 1.5 per day. Tendulikar observes succinctly that, out one person out of every three people in India are poor.
3. **Sizeable income flow from agriculture:** Agriculture is the sole source of sustenance for 60% of population in India.
4. **Deplorable infrastructural bottlenecks:** One dark spot in the body of rural India is the alarming deficiency of in infrastructural facilities like roads communication net works, banks, godown's and electricity.
5. **Conservative outlook and diverse socio-economic backwardness:** The stumbling block in the path of successful retail marketing in India is the traditional

outlook of Indian that repudiates change. The people of the country hail from varied socio, cultural and religious backgrounds.

RECENT INITIATIVES OF GOVERNMENT

Plan exercises have allowed 50 per cent retail for single brand retailing up to 100 per cent. FDI is permitted under the automatic route in whole sale cash and trading, including business to business trade and export trading up to 100 per cent. FDI is permitted with prior government approval in the trading of items sourced from the small scale sector and for test marketing. For all other activities, no FDI is permitted. Public authorities patronize store chains run by Khadi and Village Industries Commission. Textile sector is the heroe in the dram of retail market, with the entry of companies like Bombay Dyeing, and Raymonds. In the past years, doors were let open in retail agri-business for multinational companies like, Tata, PCM Shriram and Godrej. Above all, the public distribution system, at country level is operating with countries ration shops for affecting scale of essentials to the rural masses and purchase of essentials like paddy, wheat, ragi, tamarind etc. from the growers.

Retail business magnets in the country, like Kishore Biyani got inspiration for business from San Walton the iconic founder of retail changes in U.S. Kishore Biyani has started with a moderate retail trade of 200 trousers per day and the modern business has reached the level of 30 lakhs modern retails country wide in 1997.

The prerequisites for successful business specified by Kishore Biyani are given below:

> There is a balance between confidence making and a choice and humility in learning. Once you take a decision keep moving fast. Sanwalton has never followed existing pattern of his time, he studied market and developed a model. Retail business

requires space of late, there has been escalation in the prices of real estates and sky-rocketing rents of buildings is a barrier in the progress of business.

For us, writes Biyani it was customers, who matters competition is still emerging and customer is going to change rapidly.

In order to enable retail business to more steady fast prosperity we should merge look and feel of mandis with modern retail features like quality, choice and convenience. The best value for money is an environment in which the consumer is comfortable. Often Indians in cities believe that modern retail chains are expensive and avoid such places.

RETAIL MEDIA

Retail media is a novel concept in India, but it is an effective advertising platform to communicate with customers directly. TV, Radio, Advertisement, Newspaper, Branding and communication with customers are some powerful means for acquiring massive sales in market. Communicating with the Indian customer is rather tricky affair, due to diverse habits customs tastes and languages of people.

The Indian market opportunity can be segmented into different tiers. The global product market represents customers that are other multinational companies as well as selected Indian customers who are willing to pay global prices for products and services. In the global tier we include customers who are reluctant to pay global prices but seek products that are close to global standards. The local tier represents customers who are complacent with less sophisticated and often low quality products and services but offered at local prices that are much cheaper than global prices. Bulk of country's growing middle class epitomize local tier, with some moving up to the glacier tier. The bottom of pyramid includes customers who have been traditionally excluded from the market. If business stays with only with the earlier tiers, we can not fight poverty. Indian companies have started offered products and services which appeal to local and bap tiers. The innovative Indian company Bharati offers world's cheapest telecommunication service at just at one per cent per minute. This service is provided by local retailers and micro entrepreneurs who sell prepaid telephone cards in every nook and corner of India. It serves the poor by the poor (Bala Chakravarty "Happy Birth Day India, Times of India, 26-01-2010).

. The birthday gift that India craves for is more business innovation.

DEBATE ON BAN ON FDI IN RETAIL TRADE

A Parliamentary Committee recommends a blankbet ban on FDI in retail trade but the experts at the Indian Council for Research on International Economic Relations contended that due to entry of FDI in unorganized retailing the was no evidence of decline in overall employment in the unorganized retail sector. Farmers benefit sizeably from director sale to organized retailers and entry of FDI into retail trade will benefit consumers as they save more on shopping. The process of FDI entry in retail trade may not have adverse effects on small manufacturer and intermediaries while big manufacturers have to encounter fierce competition. Farmers may be befitted by organized retail, as they will not only get better prices for their products but will also acquire incentives for innovation. The parliamentary committee however, argued earlier that organized retail trade may have the effect of creating massive unemployment and wipe out unorganized retail trade.

SOME DIMENSIONS OF RETAILING

Organized retail trade in India is underdeveloped and the share of organized retail trade accounts for Rs. 35,000 cr. in 2005 (4% of total trade in the country). The shares of organized retail trade to total trade are 17 per cent, 17 per cent and 85 per cent respectively in India, China and U.S.A. From single trading activity, food retailing has natured to the stage of an industry. Food retail trade is a vast segment of economic activity in our country which accounts for 50% (Rs. 3500 billion) total sales from retailing. There is uneven growth of retailing in food items and Chennai, Bangaluru and Hyderabad are fast developing as organized hubs of the nation. Among the formats of food retailers, supermarket (Food World) which offer low margin low cost high volume service, there are discount stares, specialty stores like food processing (Haldiram), fresh product outlets selling fruits and vegetables in value added packing and convenience stores which offer products at high prices near residential societies.

REFERENCES

Das, Bhagavan Food Retailing in India: Its if Growth and Trends the *Orissa Journal of Commerce*, Volume XXI, No. 7 – 2008.

Gupta, Dr. Surendra Kumar "Rural Retailing in India: A New Concept of India Incs. *Kurukshetra*, August, 2009.

Biyani, Kishore with Dipayan Vaisya *It Happened in India*, Rupa & Co, New Delhi, 2007.

Retail Trade, *Frontline* July 2009.

Several Dailies of, *Times of India*.

Several Issues and Journals of Orissa Ćommerce Association.

2

Retail Marketing in India
The Emerging Issues and Challenges

Sudhansu Sekhar Nayak*
Anil Kumar Sahu**

INTRODUCTION

Retail is a game of multiplication. Economies of scale and distribution excellence are driven by the number of stores in a country. Retail sector, has undergone significant changes and is fast emerging in the present era of privatization, globalization and liberalization (LGP). The entry of foreign investor into retail sector in India is a progressive positive measure. India is now the 9th largest retail market in the world The retail trade revolution will definitely restructure the Indian economy and the consumers, small and medium scale businessman, farmers, and the

* Sr. Faculty, Deptt. of Commerce, R.N. College, Dura, Berhampur-10, Ganjam, Orissa.

** Reader in MBA, Berhampur University, Bhanja Bihar, Berhampur, Orissa.

government would get the benefits out of retailing. The emergence of organized retailing sector would enhance growth, improve competitiveness, provide better job opportunities, offer more goods and services and develop the agriculture and related allied industries. Consumers like middle and lower middle class prefer to purchase in multiples to get price breaks. The key to success of retail trade is differentiation and consumer satisfaction, provided Indian economics and political environment play supportive role. The retail sector has been driven by better delivery models and selection of proper location catering to every class of customers. The size of the Indian retailing industry is placed at more than Rs. 9,30,000 crore. The size of the organized segment is around Rs. 30,000 crore. According to a report by the Union Ministry of Commerce and Industry, the retail sector has been growing at seven per cent per annum (based on 1999-2002 figures). Retailing in India presents a great opportunity for international retail giants like Wal-Mart or Tesco, which can set up a wide network of retail stores and get a first mover advantage in the country.

Indian markets also have witnessed some unique changes in retail trade in the form of franchise stores, specialty stores and super markets. Retailing practices introduced by Reymonds, Arvind, Pantaloon, Shopper's stop, McDonald, Woodland, Essel World, Future Group etc. are the few illustrations to quote. Global retailers combine their finely tuned value proposition with superior retailing skills, global sourcing and access to capital to create value for both their customers and shareholders.

OBJECTIVES AND METHODOLOGY OF THE STUDY

The main objectives of the study are to examine:

(i) To what extent the large retailers have advantage over the small retailers in achieving the cost reduction and making profit;

(ii) The emerging challenges,

(iii) Recent trends and opportunities of retail business in India.

The study is mainly based on conceptual analysis on retail industry and the impact on the economy. The data are mainly collected from secondary sources i.e. periodicals, journals, books, newspapers and Internet.

ORGANIZATION OF THE STUDY

The present article attempts to highlight the emergence of retail markets in India. Besides the introduction section, article is divided into eight parts. Second part provides the objectives and methodology of the study, which contains the main objectives and sources of data. Third part involves the retail sector picture of India and key retail traders in India Fourth part gives the importance of organized retail sector over unorganized retail sector. Fifth part deals with to what extent retail sector is helpful for economic development as well as employment generation. Sixth part contains the argument for FDI in India into retail sector. Seventh part deeply describes the various emerging challenges and recent trends of retail industry development in India. Last part concludes with some glaring concluding remarks.

RETAIL INDUSTRY IN INDIA

Retail business is the largest private industry as compared to other business. In India, the retail sector is the second largest employer after agriculture. India's retail industry is highly fragmented and consists predominantly of small, independent and owner-managed shops. In 2003, retail trade in India was worth Rs. 11 lakh crore and 120 lakh retail outlets. Besides, the country is also dotted with low-cost kiosks and pushcards. There has been a boom in the retail business in India owing to gradual increase in the disposable income of the middle and lower-middle class households. More and more players are venturing into the retail business in India to introduce new attractive retail formats like malls, supermarkets, discount stores, even changing the traditional look of the book stores, chemist shops, and furnishing stores. It is estimated that for every 1000 customers only 11 retail outlets are in India. But in metro like Delhi 45 retail outlets are for every 1000 customers. In U.S.A. four retail outlets are for every 1000 costumers. Singapore is known as heart and heaven of the business; there only five retail outlets are for every 1000 customers on an average. As compared to developed countries, there is more number of retail outlets in India.

Retailing in India presents a great opportunity for foreign giants, which can set up a wide network of retail stores and get a first mover advantage in the country. India's retail progress is so rapid that it has been ranked for the second in year 2006 in the Global Retail Development Index (GRDI) as the most attractive market for foreign investors to enter.

Table 2.1: Key Retailers in India

Sl. No.	Retailer	Segment Covered
1	2	3
1.	Pantaloon Retail (I) Ltd.	Value and lifestyle retailing
2.	BATA India Ltd.	Footwear
3.	RPG Retail	Value and lifestyle retailing
4.	Shoppers stop	Lifestyle retailing
5.	Lifestyle international	Lifestyle retailing
6.	Vivek ltd.	Consumer electronics.
7.	Trent Ltd.	Value and lifestyle retailing
8.	Subhiksha Trading	Discount retailing-Foods and Grocery
9.	Marigin Free	Discount retailing-Food and Grocery

(Contd...)

1	2	3
10.	Trinethra	Value retailing-Food & Grocery
11.	Niligiri's	Value retailing-Food & Grocery
12.	Raymond Ltd.	Lifestyle retailing
13.	Plramyd merchandising and Retail Ltd.	Value and lifestyle retailing
14.	Vijay sales	Consumer electronics.
15.	Globus stores	Lifestyle retailing
16.	Nalli	Speciality saree retiling
17.	Ebony	Lifestyle retailing
18.	ITC lifestyle retailing	Lifestyle retailing
19.	Business Division	Apparel brand retailing
20.	Modura Garments	Apparel brand retailing
21.	Arvind Brands	Apparel brand retailing
22.	Levi Strauss India	Music retailing
23.	Times Retail (Planet M)	Coffee beverage retailing
24.	Barista	Coffee beverage retailing
25.	Cafe coffee day	Food service retailing
26.	McDonald's	Food service retailing
27.	Pizza Hut	Mall retailing
28.	Crossroads	Mall Retailing
29.	In. Orbit	Mall Retailing
30.	Forum Mall	Mall Retailing
31.	Spencer Plaza	Mall Retailing
32.	Nirmal Lifestyle	Mall Retailing

Total retail sales area in India was estimated at 328 million sq.m. In 2001, with an average selling space of 29.4 sq.m. per outlet. In India, per capita retailing space is about 2 sq.ft, which is quite low as compared to that of the developed economies. In 2000, the Global Management

Consultancy At Kearny put retail trade at Rs. 4,00,000 crore (1 crore =10 million), which is expected to increase at 20 per cent per year. According to a survey by AT Kearney, an overwhelming proportion of Rs. 4,00,000 crore - retail market is unorganized. In fact, only Rs. 20,000 crore segment of the market is organized. There is no integrated supply chain management outlook in the Indian traditional retail industry. However, the retail industry in India suffers from lack of management talent and poor access to best practices.

EMERGENCE OF ORGANIZED RETAIL SECTOR

One of the most dramatic changes taking place in India is in the retail sector with the emergence of organized retail sector. Organized retailing in India represents a small fraction of the total retail market. Legal procedures such as time-consuming process in title clearance, requirement of numerous lease deeds in the case of multiple ownership, and difficulties in conversion of normal land into commercial use are some of the basic difficulties impairing the development of organized retailing in India The developed countries' retail industry is majority organized whereas in India, it still remains unorganized. Table 2.2 shows the position of organized and unorganized retail industry of some countries.

Table 2.2: Organized Retail Industry Globally

Sl. No.	Control	Size (US $ Billion)	Organized Retail Industry	Traditional Retail Industry
1.	USA	2,325	85%	15%
2.	Taiwan	115	81%	19%
3.	Malaysia	20	55%	45%
4.	Thailand	22	40%	60%
5.	Brazil	100	36%	64%
6.	Indonesia	75	30%	70%
7.	Poland	55	20%	80%
8.	China	325	20%	80%
9.	India	180	02%	98%

Source: Marketing White Book 2005.

In USA and Taiwan, the share of organized retail industry is 85 and 81 per cent respectively whereas in India, it is only two per cent. The main reasons for low organized retail business in India are:

(i) Family business and conducted unprofessionally,

(ii) Legal restriction,

(iii) Finance catering to a limited target of people etc..

But organized retailing business in semi-urban areas and larger cities is growing at 50%-60% and 35%-40% respectively in India, because of its current nascent stage and the investments planned in this sector by existing and new players. It is estimated that the organized retail market will be 20 per cent of total retailing by end of 2008.

The four major segments which will grow in the organized Indian retail sectors, are Food, Clothing, Consumer Durables and Books and Music. Table 2.3 indicates their estimated size and projections.

Table 2.3: Size of the Organized Retail Market (Rs. Cr.)

Segment	2001-02	2007	CAGR(%)
Total	16,000	37,216	18
Food	1,800	7,473	33
Consumer durables	1,650	3,787	18
Clothing	4,950	10,423	16
Books and Music	450	1,426	26

Sources: Changing Gears, The Economic Times, Intelligence Group.

In the following section, let's analyze prominent sectors in Indian retail with respect to the composition of the sector, key players and the estimated size of the market. Since the exact figures for the industry and its various segments are not available, the size and projected growth of the sectors have been taken from the images.

KS A INDIA RETAIL REPORT - 2005

Retail Industry—GDP and Employment

Retail industry is one of the largest private industries in India. In India, 5 lakh people are engaged in organized retail sector and 4 crore people are engaged in unorganized retail sector. This is the picture of Indian retail industry. If organized retail industry grows into a ful-fledged industry, it will require a more sophisticated set of store staff and professionals at managerial level. The requirement is expected to gather momentum and employment in this sector would go up to as high as 20 per cent. Thus the retailing would be unmatched in terms of its potential for employment generation, both in numbers and quality of professionalism. Table 2.4 shows the share of retailing to the GDP and its contribution total employment.

Table 2.4: Retail Industry's Contribution to GDP and Employment

Sl. No.	Country	Share in GDP (%)	Share in Employment (%)
1.	USA	9.4	16.7
2.	Poland	11.0	14.7
3.	China	8.0	12.0
4.	India	10.0	6.0
5.	Brazil	6.4	6.0

Source: CII-Mckinsey Report.

It is revealed from the table that the share of retailing in India's GDP stands at 10 per cent and its share in employment is only at 6 per cent. It is mainly due to unorganized retail industry.

FDI IN INDIAN RETAIL INDUSTRY

India replaced Russia to move from second place to first in 2005 and 2006, Global Retail Development Index (GRDI) released by AT Kearney recently. The index is a measure of retail investment attractiveness among 30 emerging markets across the globe. This indicates that India is the most attractive market for investments flowing into retail Industry. A Government Commissioned Report produced on behalf of the Ministry of Consumers Affairs has advocated opening of the retail sector to FDI with players like Wal-Mart allowed owning 49 per cent of the retail ventures, in a timeframe of 3 to5 years. Retailing has already been looked at a prospective area for FDI. The Government is also promoting investment in supply chains and infrastructure like real estate through FDI to facilitate retail growth.

Let's take an example; in just 10 years after China permitted FDI in the retail sector, the share of organized retail business has been increased to 20 per cent from 10 per cent. The FDI is a method of allowing external finance into economy. The FDI also facilitates foreign trade and transfer of knowledge, skills and technology. The Tenth Plan approach paper postulates a GDP growth rate of 8 per cent during 2002-07. This implies an increase in FDI from the present level of $3.9 billion in 2001-02 to at least around US $ 8 billion a year, during 2002-07. India is the vast emerging place for FDI, according to the FDI Confidence Index prepared by AT Kearney. India ranks second in FDI after China. Table 2.5 shows the top FDI destinations.

Franchising of operations appears to be the most popular strategy followed by the international retailers for entry into India. Under this method, the parent company lends its name and technology to a local partner and gets royalty in return. The other route for entry is a joint venture, whereby the international giant provides equity and support to the India investor and the Indian partner provides all the local knowledge that is typically needed for such a venture. Mc Donalds and Reebok have adopted the joint venture route in India. It is argued that FDI will increase volumes in turnover which would convert into more production, more employment in industry and more prosperity. So in order to reap the maximum benefits from FDIs, there is a need to establish in transparent, board and effective policy environment for investments and to put in place, an appropriate framework for their implementation. Gradually opening up of retail industry for FDI, both the customers as well as existing retailers will take advantages. While customers will have variety of global branded goods and services to choose from and that too a reachable cost and the existing retailers will be saddled with a host of unseen opportunities like joint ventures with foreign giants apart from avenue to upgrade there technologies, systems etc.

Table 2.5: Key FDI Destinations

Sl. No	Country	Rank 2005	Rank 2004
1.	China	1	1
2.	India	2	3
3.	USA	3	2
4.	UK	4	4
5.	Poland	5	1
6.	Russia	6	11
7.	Brazil	7	17
8.	Australia	8	7
9.	Germany	9	5
10.	Hong Kong	10	8

Source: AT Kearney, *The Times of India,* December 9,2005.

THE EMERGING CHALLENGES TO RETAIL INDUSTRY'S DEVELOPMENT IN INDIA

Organized retail sector in India is little over a decade old. It is largely an urban phenomenon and the pace of growth is still slow. Some of the reasons for this slow growth are:

(i) Retail sector not recognized as an industry in India

(ii) The high costs of real estate.

(iii) High stamp duties

(iv) Lack of adequate infrastructure and adequate knowledge.

(v) Multiple and complex taxation system

(vi) Lack of strategic planning, advanced marketing skills and financial resources etc.

Yet, few can deny that India today provides on of the biggest consumption opportunities in the world. The consensus is that the macro trends in urbanization, demographics shifts and income growth will be positives and irreversible. At the projected Indian GDP growth in the next five years, and allowing for an inflation of 3 to 4 per cent, the nominal per capita income is expected to double from $ 600 to $ 1200. This implies that the consumption and the retailing opportunities will also double from its existing market size of $ 250 billion. Behind this rising in consumption, there are three important enablers that can be traced to the demographic profile of our country. These are:

1. We are one of the youngest nations in the world, a demographic characteristic that even betters the state of China.

2. The second factor is the participation of Indian women in workforce.

3. The third most important factor is the emergence of entirely new set of urban and semi-urban customers who have not yet been tapped by modem organized retail and most consumer companies in India.

The five forces (MICHAL PORTER) together determine the intensity of industry competition and profitability. Let's consider each of the five forces with respect to the Indian retail sector.

Entry of Competitors

The ease of entity for competitors to enter the market and to start competing and the barriers to entry, which may exist. There exist the high threats, i.e. regulation on FDI, building up economies of scale, substantial capital requirements, distribution strategies, product differentiation etc. of new entrants in this sector.

Threat of Substitutes

The ease with which a product or a service can be substituted, especially made cheaper. In Indian retail, the threat of substitutes is very high. The unorganized retailing in India still the largest wherein cheaper versions of products are available. This still services most of the middle and poor incomes families in the country.

Bargaining Power of Buyers

The position of the buyers, can they work together to gain efficiencies in buying? In Indian retail, the bargaining power of buyers is fast increasing and can be termed as moderate to high, depending on the product or service. The buyers are most powerful in the retailing industry, hi an age of the informed consumer, meeting buyer's expectations in terms of product, price and service is increasingly becoming difficult.

Bargaining Power of Suppliers

The position of the sellers. Do many suppliers exist or is there a existence of only a few suppliers? The suppliers to the retailing industry are the companies who provide the finished products to make various retail products. The bargaining power of suppliers varies from the product supplies. The bargaining power of suppliers is low because there are a large number of potential supplies in the market. Therefore the prices become competitive.

Rivalry Among the Existing Players

The level of competition between the existing players, the size and the strength of the players in the industry. The intensity of rivalry between competitors in an industry depends on the structure of the competition for example, rivalry is more intense where there are many small or equally sized competitors; rivalry is less when an industry has a clear market leader. The structure of the industry costs, the degree of the differentiation and the switching costs determine the intensity of rivalry in any industry.

The five forces model is a strategic tool that is used to analysis the attractiveness and development of the retail industry structure.

CONCLUSION

A look at the landscape of most cities in India shows the rapid pace of change. This change is a reflection of the changes on the Indian consumer, his life style and his habits. In India, retail business is the new buzzword. The need of the hour for Indian retail business is to develop systems and processes keeping the unique nature of the country in mind. Retailers must be aware about good customer service, so that they not only increase and attract retail customers but also customers delight can be achieved which is an asset to the company. Retailing posed with booming business opportunities in appeals, fashions, restaurants, Jewellery, furniture and home decor, grocery and culleries and variety of consumer durables and even service retailing like banks, postal, telephones, public service, courier, credit cards, hotel etc. FDI in retail industry would certainly enable to optimize youth employment in India. The Government of India should further liberalize the FDI norms for retail industry. It may create a healthy competition among local and international retail traders to offer superior quality products at reasonable rates. The retail industries will create more job employment and enhance the GDP. Information Technology (IT) also makes it easier to open stores as well as develop systems to aid local store managers and to manage thousands of stores spread all over the world. The retail industry will be more beneficial in the areas like development of agricultural and processed food industry, improvement of supply chain management, development of tourism industry, greater exports, increase hi tax revenues etc. With the emergence of large and new form of retailing after liberalization, Indian consumers started gaining from this market This type of practice is new to the Indian consumers. But last, but not the least, nobody wants to miss out of retailing business in India.

REFERENCES

Indian Retail Review, Vol. I, January-2007, Birla Institute of Management Technology, Noida.

Indian Retail Review, Vol. I, December 2007, Birla Institute of Management Technology, Noida.

The Hindu, Survey of Indian Industry-2006.

The Hindu, Survey of Indian Industry-2007.

Bajaj, Chetan, *Retail Management* - Rajnish Tuli, Nidhi V Srivastava. Oxford Higher Education.

Pradhan, Swapna, *Retailing Management - Text and Cases*. The Tata McGraw-Hill Companies

3

Retail Industry in India
Trends, Challenges and Prospects

Prabin Kumar Padhy*

INTRODUCTION

Retailing in one of the India's largest industries employing 8 per cent of the workforce next to agriculture. It supplements over 10 per cent of GDP in India. The post-liberalization era, saw retail industry undergoing a revolutionary change. In the global scenario, marketing era has evolved on account of economic and business pressure which emphasized on adopting a number of managerial measures so as to satisfy consumer needs and earns their long term loyalty. The importance of Marketing within the retail industry can be attributed to:

- The level of economic growth throughout the twentieth century.
- Improvement in the standard of living.

* Head, Deptt. of Management, Gayatri Institute of Science and Technology, Berhampur. Orissa.

- Increase in the population.
- Improvement in the educational standard of the people.
- Increase in the discretionary time of the consumers.
- Changing demographics and industrial structure
- Expanding computer technology
- Emphasis on lower costs and prices
- Emphasis on convenience and service.
- Focus on productivity
- Added experimentation
- High disposable income among the people
- Good infrastructure
- High level of awareness of quality, and brand consciousness of the customers
- Willingness and eagerness to spend
- A growing urban youth population.

OBJECTIVES AND METHODOLOGY OF THE STUDY

1. To analyze in detail the development of retail business in various parts of the world.
2. The emerging challenges.
3. Recent trends and opportunities of retail business in India.

The study is mainly based on conceptual analysis on retail industry and the impact on the economy. The data are mainly collected from the secondary sources.

STRUCTURE OF THE STUDY

The present article attempts to highlight the emergence of retail markets in India. Besides the introductory section the article is divided into eight parts. The second section provides the objectives and methodology of the study, which contains the main objectives and sources of data. Third section deals with the Concepts, of Retail trade, Fourth section gives in detail, Retail industry in North America, Economic Union, Europe, and other developed countries. The fifth section deals with the Retail Industry trends. It also discusses the size of retail industry in the world economies, GDP and employment of people in retailing. The sixth section elaborates prospects of retailing. The seventh section discusses the emerging challenges in Retail Industry and Concluding remarks.

CONCEPTS OF RETAILING

The world 'Retailing' has been derived from the old French word 'Retailer' meaning 'a piece of' or to cut a piece off or to break a bulk. This can be applied to the functions carried out by the retailer–acquiring whole stock of goods which they divide into smaller amounts which are sold to individual consumers. David Gilbert has defined retail as "Any business that directs its marketing efforts towards the satisfying the final consumer based upon the organization, of selling goods and services as a means of distribution". According to Michael Ley Bandon A Weiz: The retailing is the set of business activities which adds values to the products and services sold to consumers for the personal or family use. So, from the above mentioned definitions. Retailers are referred to as middlemen, intermediaries because they occupy a middle position in the distribution channel. They receive goods from producers, and wholesalers, and pass on to the consumers. The retailers are able to accomplish, this through the store/retail outlet located at a convenient place and ensure that customers are focal-point, for the selection and display of stock. Simply said: Retailing involves various activities of shopping such as purchasing through the internet, dealing in financial services, eating at restaurant, visiting the beauty parlour. A retailer is a part of the supply chain for any product that it sells. A retailer comes at the end of supply chain and provides the final link between consumer and producer. Retailers attempt to satisfy consumer needs by having right merchandise at right price, at right time and at right place wher the consumer wants. While going through the retail chain linking customers and producers they perform the functions such as:

(i) providing an assortment of products and services;

(ii) breaking the bulk;

(iii) holding inventories;

(iv) providing services;

(v) increasing the value of products and services.

RETAIL INDUSTRY IN NORTH AMERICA, ECONOMIC UNION, EUROPE

Retail is the second largest industry in the United States in terms of both the number of establishments and the number of employees. It is also one of the largest industries worldwide. The retail industry employs over 23 million Americans and generates more than $ 3 trillion in retail sector annually. Wal-Mart is world's largest retailer and the largest company with approximately US $ 245 billion, in sales annually. Wal-Mart employs more than one million associates in the United States and more than 3,00,000 internationally. The second largest retailer in the world is France's Carrefour, Single Store Business account for over 95 per cent of the US retailers, but generates less than 50 per cent of all retail store sales. Some two-thirds or US $ 6.6 trillion out of the US $ 10 trillion. American economy is consumer spending about 40 per cent of that $ 3 trillion spent on discretionary products and services. Retail turnover in the Economic Union was almost 2,000 billion in 2001 and the sectors better than average looks set to continue in the future. Retail trade in Europe employs 15 per cent of the European workforce and 12 million workers. The Asian Economies (excluding Japan) are expected to have 6 per cent growth rates in 2005-06.

Global Retail Industry related facts:

- Worldwide retail sales are estimated at US $ 7 trillion.

- The top 200 largest retailers account for 35 per cent of worldwide demand
- The money spent on household consumption, worldwide increased by 68 per cent between 1980 and 1998.

RETAILERS WORLDWIDE AND INDIAN RETAILERS

Some of the giant foreign multinational retail traders are Wal-Mart, Mc Donald, Kroger, Home Depot, Albertson, Sears, Safeway, of USA, Tesco & Sainsbury of UK, Carrefour, Intermarche of France,Metro of Germany, Ahold of Netherlands, Ho-Yakudu of Japan. Organised retailing in India is very less i.e only two per cent of the total retail business, whereas unorganized is 98 per cent, in contrast to the USA, where organized business is 85 per cent in Taiwan 81 per cent and Malaysia 55 per cent. In those countries the organized retailing is more than the unorganized business, The types of retail industrial practices in some of the countries and their size of business and percentage share of each is displayed in Table 3.1.

Table 3.1: Retail Industry Types, Country, and Size of Business

Sl. No.	Country	Size of Retail Business (US $ Billion)	Organized Retail Industry	Traditional Retail Industry
1.	USA	2,325	85%	15%
2.	Taiwan	115	81%	19%
3.	Malayasia	20	55%	45%
4.	Thailand	22	40%	60%
5.	Brazil	100	36%	64%
6.	Indonesia	75	30%	70%
7.	Poland	55	20%	80%
8.	China	325	20%	80%
9.	India	180	02%	98%

Source: Marketing White Book 2005.

Retail business is the largest private industry as compared to other business. In India the the retail sector is the second largest employer after agriculture. India's retail industry is highly fragmented and consists of predominantly small, independent, and owner managed shops. The country is dotted with low cost kiosks, and push cards.

RETAIL INDUSTRY - GDP AND EMPLOYMENT

In India five lakhs of people are engaged in organized retail sector and four crores of people are engaged in unorganized retail sector. If organized retail sector grows into a full fledged industry, it will require a more sophisticated set of more staff and professionals at managerial level. The requirements are expected to gather momentum and employment in this sector would grow at a high rate as high as 20 per cent. Thus the retailing would be unmatched in terms of its potential for employment generation both in number and quality of professionalis, Table 3.2 shows the share of retailing to the GDP and its contribution to total employment. It is revealed from the table that the share of retailing in India's GDP stands at 10 per cent and share of employment is eight per cent. Out of which 98 per cent are unorganized retail outlets.

Table 3.2: Retail Industry's Contribution to GDP and Employment

Sl. No.	Country	Share of GDP	Share in employment
1.	USA	9.4	16.7
2.	Poland	11.0	14.7
3.	China	8.0	12.0
4.	India	10.0	8.0
5.	Brazil	6.4	6.0

Source: Mckinsey Report.

It is estimated that for every 1000 customers only 11 retail outlets are in India. But in metro cities like Delhi 45 retail outlets are for every 1000 customers. In U.S.A., four retail outlets are for every 1000 customers. Singapore is known as heart and heaven of the business. There are only five retail outlets for every 1000 customers on an average. As compared to the developed countries India is having more number of retail outlets in India. Retailing in India presents a great opportunity for foreign giants, by which they can set up a wide range of network of retail stores

RETAIL INDUSTRY IN INDIA

According to the Global Retail Development Index (GRDI), 2006 determined by the Management consulting Firms A.T. Kearney, the Indian market has retained the top position in the annual study of retailed investments attractiveness among 30 countries. As a part of research A.T. Kearney, conducted a voice of the Global retailer's survey in order to understand what they consider as the key success factors while expanding outside their home markets. It was found that global retailers identify emerging countries on the basis of country risk, market attractiveness, market saturation, time pressures etc. Some of the key retailers in India are as given in Table 3.3.

Table 3.3: Key Retailers in India

Sl. No.	Retailer's Name	Segment Covered
1	2	3
1.	Pantaloon Retail(I) Ltd.	Value and lifestyle retailing
2.	Bata India Limited	Footwear, Garments
3.	RPG Retail	Value and lifestyle retailing
4.	Shoppers Stop	Value and lifestyle retailing
5.	Lifestyle International	Value and lifestyle retailing
6.	Vivek Ltd.	Consumer electronics
		(Contd...)

1	2	3
7.	Trent Ltd.	Value and lifestyle retailing
8.	Subhiksha Trading	Discount retailing-Food & Grocery
9.	Marigin Free	Discount retailing-Food & Grocery
10.	Trinethra	Value retailing-Food & Grocery
11	Nilgiri's	Value retailing-Food & Grocery
12.	Raymonds Limited	Value and lifestyle retailing
13.	Pyramid merchandising and retail Ltd.	Value and lifestyle retailing
14.	Vijay Sales	Consumer electronics
15.	Globus Stores	Value and lifestyle retailing
16.	Nalli	Speciality Saree retailing
17.	Ebony	Value and lifestyle retailing
18.	ITC lifestyle retailing	Value and lifestyle retailing
19.	Business Division	Apparel Brand Retailing
20.	Madura Garments	Apparel Brand Retailing
21.	Arvind Brands	Apparel Brand Retailing
22.	Levi Strauss India	Music retailing
23.	Times Retail (Planet M)	Coffee Beverage retailing
24.	Barista	Coffee Beverage retailing
25.	Café Coffee Day	Food service retailing
26.	Mc Donald's	Food service retailing
27.	Pizza Hut	Mall retailing
28.	Crossroads	Mall retailing
29.	In Orbit	Mall retailing
30.	Forum Mall	Mall retailing
31.	Spencer Plaza	Mall retailing
32.	Nirmal Lifestyle	Mall retailing

TRENDS OF RETAILING

Today, India is in the midst of retail revolution. Besides other factors, rising income and increasing consumerism are fuelling the retail growth in the country.

Table 3.4: Indian Retail Landscape

Year	Retail Trade in Billion $
1998	201
2000	204
2002	238
2004	278
2006	321
2008	368
2010*	421

Source: A.T. Kearney, Report on Retail India.

Table 3.4 indicates the magnitude of retail trade in India. The retail trade, which was US $ 201 billion in 1998 is estimated to touch US $ 368 billion in the year 2008 and U.S. $ 421 billion in 2010. The Global Retail Development Index (GRDI), a measure of global retail attractiveness among 32 emerging markets, released by global market consultancy firm A.T. Kearney. It reveals that India has moved from second place to first place by displacing Russia in 2005. This indicates that India is the most attractive destination for directing investments into the retail sector.

The above paras found that India was seen as an attractive emerging market, occupying second position after Russia, offering similar potential to that revealed by China 15 years ago. As far as the retail industry is concerned, India is standing at the brink of a great economic opportunity. In the Goldman BRIC (Brazil, Russia, India, and China) Report, India is predicted to be amongst the top three economies in the world by 2050, along with China and Brazil. While, the Tata Group Economic Survey predicts, that there will be a total of 75 million households under the consuming classes category with an annual income level of $ 1,000-$4,800 by the year 2005-06. The organized retail sector in India is expected to grow from the existing two per cent of the total retail industry to five per cent per annum, and by 20 per cent by the end of decade. In Asia the retail market is evolving and India ha s moved up to the second place, just behind China. Between 1999-2003 periods India's GDP has increased by 40 per cent.

The other contributory factor for the growth of retail sector is the rising proportion of young population. More than 52 per cent of its population is less than 25 years of age which is demographic dividend. India is going to reap from its young population. Hence there is a demographic transition in the economy. There has been a boom in the retail business in India owing to gradual increase in the disposable income of the middle and lower middle class households.

The middle class population in India is around 480 million with monthly household income ranging from US $ 150 to $ 1,000. Further the average household income in urban areas has grown at five per cent CAGR (Compound Annual Growth Rate) over the past decade.

Indian Retail Report 2009, compiled by Research Group Images that spiraling income and rising economic growth of the industry and it will touch Rs. 18,10,000 crores by 2010. Organised retail is expected to constitute 12 per cent of it, i.e (Rs. 2,30,000 crores) . The people feel that organized retail will it many but modernized retail will generate employment for 15 million people in different activities. Out of which Food, grocery will be 59.5 per cent amounting to Rs. 7,92,000 crores.Clothing and accessories will be 9.9 per cent amounting to 1,31,300 crores.

According to KSA Techno Park's Consumer Outlook 2004 report that estimates that the average Indian spends 40 per cent of his monthly salary on food and grocery. According to this year's Global Retail Development Index India is positioned as the leading destination for retail investment. This followed from the saturation in Western retail market and we find big Western retailers like Wal-Mart and Tesco entering into Indian market. India's retail industry accounts for 10 per cent of GDP and 8 per cent of employment. to reach $ 17 billion by 2010. There are about 300 new malls, 1,500 supermarkets and 325 departmental stores.

A shopping revolution is ushering in India, where a large population between (20-34) age group in the urban regions is boosting demand by 11.1 per cent in 2004-05 to an Rs. 23,308 purchasing power. This has resulted in large international retail investment and a more liberal Foreign direct investment. Organised retail will form 10 per cent of total retailing by the end of 2010. From 2006-2010, the organized sector will grow at the Compound Annual Growth Rate (CAGR), around 49.53 per cent.

PROSPECTS OF RETAILING

1. Retailing will create millions of jobs for all the young educated men and women that pour out of colleges.
2. The retail industry is the most sophisticated users of technology. The growth of Wal-Mart and Dell is simply because they manage the best global supply chains.
3. Retail markets reduce the costs by operating and procurements leverage. They score the world looking for cheaper and high quality products.
4. Opening of large numbers of big retailers can improve the quality of the products, bring higher income to the producer, and lower price of the consumer goods.
5. Increase in the number of talented people to plan for merchandise in logistics and to manage the supply chain, information, stores.

6. **Benefits to Overall Economy:** Retailing contributes to GDP and creates employment opportunities and produces talented people to run the business.
7. Product innovation and growth of infrastructure.
8. Franchising opportunity for local entrepreneur.
9. Investment in Supply Chain, cold chain and Warehousing.

THE EMERGING CHALLENGES TO RETAIL INDUSTRY'S DEVELOPMENT IN INDIA

Organized retail sector in India is little over a decade old. It is largely an urban phenomenon and the pace of growth is still slow. Some of the reasons for this slow growth are:

1. Retail sector is not recognized as an industry in India.
2. The high cost of real estate.
3. High stamp duties.
4. Lack of adequate infrastructure.
5. Multiple and complex taxation systems.
6. Lack of strategic planning, advanced marketing skills, and financial resources.
7. Entry of competitors.
8. Threat of Substitutes.
9. Bargaining power of buyers.
10. Bargaining power of suppliers.
11. Rivalry among the existing players.
12. Lack of trained manpower.
13. Impact of organized retailers.
14. Innovation in the products.
15. The Global Challenges from the global retailers.

CONCLUSION

The retail boom has to strive in India. It will bring lucrative career to the young, money to the producer and profit margin to the seller, revenues to the government, and will bring economic development in our country. To keep pace with development and face stiff competition from global retailers, the retailers of India have to improve their quality, cost, marketability and managerial skill. Decision-makers must adopt policies to encourage upcoming retailers and frame such policies, rules and regulations which will foster entrepreneurship. Retailers must be able to decide where to move, when, how much to invest, and entering a new market .Entrepreneurs have to given incentives for entering into the business and necessary support and training and financial support should be given.

REFERENCES

Bajaj, C. Tuli R., and Shrivastava Nidhi, *Retail Management*, Oxford University Press, New Delhi, 2006.

Berman, B and Evans-J.R, *Retail Management: A Strategic, Approach*, 9th Edition, Prentice-Hall of India Pvt. Ltd., New Delhi.

Indian Retail Report 2009-10.

Nair, Suja R, *Retail Management*.

Pradhan, Swapna, *Retailing Management*–Text and Cases. The Tata McGraw-Hill Companies.

Organized and Unorganized Retail Sector and Customer Preference in India

Nilima Das*
Sudhakar Patra**

ABSTRACT

Retailing is the activity of selling goods and services to a final consumer for his/her own use. Retailers form the link between manufacturers, wholesalers, agents, and the customers. They are the persons who keep in touch with the customers and get an opportunity to understand their needs and preferences. The purpose of this article to analyze the customer and what they generally perceive while they are purchasing products. This article also describes differences between organized retail sector and unorganized retail sector and also highlights the growth of retail sector in India. In this article the causes of preferring organized retail

* Lecturer in Marketing, Trident Academy of Creative Technology, Bhubaneswar, Orissa.

** Reader in Economics, Ravenshaw University, Cuttack, Orissa.

shop/unorganized retail shop some factors which influence customer preference are discussed.

INTRODUCTION

The Indian retail market, which is the fifth largest retail destination globally, has been ranked as the most attractive emerging market for investment in the retail sector by AT Kearney's Eighth Annual Global Retail Development Index (GRDI), in 2009. As per a study conducted by the Indian Council for Research on International Economic Relations (ICRIER), the retail sector is expected to contribute to 22 per cent of India's GDP by 2010. A McKinsey report, 'The Rise of Indian Consumer Market', estimates that the Indian consumer market is likely to grow four times by 2025. Commercial real estate services company, CB Richard Ellis' findings state that India's retail market has moved up to the 39th most preferred retail destination in the world in 2009, up from 44 Past year.

According to a report by Northbride Capita, the India retail industry is expected to grow to US$ 700 billion by 2010. By the same time, the organized sector will be 20 per cent of the total market share. It can be mentioned here that, the share of organized sector in 2007 was 7.5 per cent of the total retail market.

Retailing refers to all activities involved in selling the products and services to the ultimate consumers. Retailing is the world's largest private sector contributing to eight per cent of the GDP and it employs one sixth of the labor force. Many countries have developed only due to retailing and presently there is a vast change in the retail industry. In India, it contributes to 14 per cent of our GDP and it is the second largest sector next to agriculture which provides employment to more number of persons. According to a survey, India is classified in to the fifth most attractive retail destination and second among the countries in Asia.

Worldwide it is ranked as fifth most attractive retail destination. Retailing is supposed to provide Product Utility, Place Utility, Time Utility and Ownership Utility.

It provides final end products to the consumers, not raw materials, end products in usable form to the consumers. Thereby it creates product utility. Second one, it is given in the place where it is required by the consumer. That is, retailing outlets are open in the places according to the convenience of the customer and also based on the demand of the consumer. Third One, it creates Time Utility. Whenever the consumers want to go and shop they can go and shop at a particular period convenient to the customer. Next one, when the product is sold finally it creates Ownership Utility. So, we can conclude that retailing is a marketing intermediary which creates Product Utility, Place Utility, Time Utility and Ownership Utility in providing goods and services to the consumers.

OBJECTIVES OF THE STUDY

This research article has following objectives:

1. To analyze customer buying behaviour.
2. To analyze differentiation between organized and unorganized sector.
3. To examine the factors driving customers towards organized/unorganized retail shop.
4. To analyze causes of dissatisfaction of customer with organized/unorganized retail shop.
5. To examine the psychology of consumers what they think, feel, while selecting between different alternatives (e.g., brands, products).
6. To understand the psychology of the consumers and nature of influence by his or her environment (e.g., culture, family, signs, media)

CLASSIFICATION AND FUNCTIONS OF RETAIL SECTOR

Retail Sector can be classified into two segments such as organized segment and unorganized segment. In India, this organized segment contributes only to 3 per cent of the retail trade and the unorganized segment contributes to remaining 97 per cent of the retail trade. This is because people purchasing only from the street vendors and from the local shops and organized retailing was not popular in India. After 1991, due to liberalization and globalisation, this organized sector has come to light and presently it exists in various formats such as Super markets, Hypermarkets, Departmental stores and Specialty stores.

Retail marketing plans, sales promotion ideas, branding and advertising resources for retailers can promote retailing in India. Participating in area activities not only helps promote brand awareness, it can also leave a retailer feeling good for giving something back to a supportive community. When the economy starts sputtering that's when savvy retailers take action. Every newspaper, news program, news website is full of doom and gloom these days. Stores closings, foreclosures, rising gas prices, job cuts, rising food prices are all the top stories in the media. Small business owners can easily get too involved in the day-to-day operations of their retail stores to spend any time brainstorming marketing ideas. Some retailers worry that marketing is too expensive, others may find it too time consuming. Many states across the nation have adopted some form of tax-free holiday. The sales tax holidays are designed to offer relief to taxpayers by providing a temporary sales tax exemption on certain goods during a specific time period.

Studies of customer behaviour in retail stores usually deals with identification of customers and their buying behaviour patterns. The aim of such studies is to astern who buys, what buys, when and how. In addition such studies endeavor to learn about customer responses to sales promotion devices .The results of these studies are useful in the solution of an array of marketing problems. The "why" of customer behaviour is a separate and very difficult subject; it is not treated here. Knowledge of customer behaviour must precede any consideration of the reasons for the behaviour. First task involved is to identify who is a customer and who is a consumer? The terms 'consumer' and 'customer' are not synonymous. A customer is the purchaser of a product or a service; a consumer is a user of a product or service. The buying behaviour of the consumer is influenced by the needs and preferences of the consumer for whom the products are purchased. Marketers primarily concerned with customers' buying behaviour rather than with the consumers preferences. Identification of customers seeks to ascertain who the customers are. It is not sufficient to study buying behaviour pattern without knowing whose buying behaviour is involved. Hence, it is necessary to identify the composition and origin of customer.

COMPOSITION OF CUSTOMERS

The composition of customer involved different types of people involves many characteristics like age, sex, race, religion, income level, status, different ethnic background and different region, state, country etc. Customer may be a 3-year grown up child or 3-month new born baby. Customer may belong to the different religion like Hindu, Muslim, Sikh, Christian etc. Marketer also observing different types of customer who are belongs to different income level. Some customer may switch over to another brand due their preferences. Some of customer became loyal to a particular product. To understand a customer mind is difficult task for a marketer. Marketers generally consider customer mind is black box. Composition of customer also involves different roles plays by customer like initiator, influencer, purchaser, influencer, decider, user etc. decision-making with regard to retail outlet selection is very similar to consumer decision-making on brands where the consumer goes through a process starting from identifying needs to post-purchase issues. There are a few interesting and important dimensions associated with consumer behaviour and retail outlet selection.

ORGANIZED RETAIL SECTOR VS. UNORGANIZED RETAIL SECTOR

The current scenario of retail sector in India is changing. Previously, customers used to go to *kirana* stores to purchases their necessities. This later changed to bigger shops run by one man with a few employees. Here, all the work was done manually. Gradually, more sophistication seeped into this sector and department stores came into being. Beginning in the mid-1990s, however, there was an explosion of shopping malls and plazas where customers interacted with professionals and not with just one single person - the owner. An important point here is that customers' requirements are catered to by trained staff. Today, organized retailing has become an experience characterized by comfort, style and speed. It is something that offers a customer more control, convenience and choice along with an experience.

Retail sector is basically divided into two types Organized sector and Unorganized sector. Organized retail refers to the traditional formats of low-cost retailing, for example, the local *kirana* shops; owner operated general stores, *paan/beedi* shops, convenience stores, hand cart and pavement vendors, etc. Organized retail means trading activities undertaken by licensed retailers, that is, those who are registered for sales tax, income tax, etc. These include the corporate-backed hypermarkets and retail chains, and also the privately owned large retail businesses. In India around 97 per cent-98 per cent of the retail industry is unorganized. Among the organized ones the already established corporate retailers in India are Pantaloon Retail, Shoppers' Stop, Spencers, Hyper city, Lifestyle, Subhiksha and

Reliance Retail etc. Traditional unorganized retail is expected to face tough times to withstand against modern, organized retail which now constitutes a small four per cent of total retail sector. The organized retail is likely to grow at a much faster pace of 45-50 per cent per annum and quadruple its share in total retail trade to 16 per cent by 2011-12. Government is also apprehensive about the uncertain future of this sector.

PREFERENCE TO PURCHASE FROM ORGANIZED RETAIL SECTOR

India is one of the most over-populated retail destinations in the world with one outlet for every 100 persons. Around 95 per cent of shopping is from the neighbourhood retailer who offers convenience, credit and personalized service—so why would consumers switch to modern formats which offer little differentiation in pricing (in the absence of scale or superior logistics) or location (convenience store formats like Subhiksha or Reliance Fresh are proving unviable)? Below we are discussing some arguments in favor of why people prefer to purchase from organized retail sector.

1. The consumer buys from these outlets because he gets the right quality at a lower price. Outlets such as Big Bazaar, Reliance Retail, Subhiksha and The World (a well known organized shopping mall of Orissa) have been delivering quality produce at lower prices.
2. The range of products organized retail offers is something that customer do not find in a mom-and-pop store". For example very expensive products like Sehnaz Husen beauty products. Mom and Pop shops are not interested to keep costly products due to the fear may be they are not able to sell costly products.
3. Working couple prefer organized retail for the sheer range of products they can access easily there. Working

couple do not have much time for standing in front of *kirana* shop or mom-and-pop shop. So it's a better for them to go a organized retail shop where they can easily search for their requirements.

4. Organized retail shop is well organized with variety of products. Generally people prefer to visit organized retail because they are able to get plenty options for their choice.
5. Many organized retail shops having good infrastructure facility. It looks neat and clean, free from crowed unorganized retail sector like vendor. So people enjoy their shopping.
6. Customer between age group 15-30 are also enjoying to visit shopping mall rather than unorganized retail shop. Shopping malls are always keeping updated products which are preferred by youngsters.
7. People who are visit outside of State or nation they also prefer to shop at organized retail sector. Because they don't have idea regarding the places as well as they want to avoid cheater.
8. In an organized retail shop the sellers are well trained and they able to communicate with local language, international language as well as national language.
9. In organized retail shop there is also facility of issue of discount card. With the help of this discount card people can purchase with some discount amount.

PREFERENCE TO PURCHASE FROM UNORGANIZED SECTOR

India is the only one country having the highest shop density in the world; with 11 outlets per 1000 people (12 million retail shops for about 209 million households). Let have a look why people prefer to purchase from unorganized sector.

1. People prefer to buy vegetables from the traditional *mandi* because of quality and low price. Customers perceived they can do good bargaining with traditional vendor which is not possible at organized retail shop.

2. People buy from the mom-and-pop stores on credit during the month and settle the bill when they receive their salaries in the first week of the succeeding month.

3. Customers are also belongs to lower stratum of society represent people who are either daily-wagers or who work for the unorganized trade and industry; their employment is seasonal which means they may remain jobless during the off-season. At sunset, they receive their wages with which they buy rice or *atta* for the austere supper ahead. Their purchases are meager and only the mom-and-pop stores will entertain them. Organized retail will not vend 50 ml of edible oil or 250 g of rice or *atta* to such humble consumers.

4. People perceived traditional vendor or *kirana* shop provides discount on regular purchases, which is normally not done by big shopping mall. Discount cards are also given by organized retail shop but due to the illiteracy of customer they are unable to know these things.

5. Those belonging to the lower end of the middle-income group are prefer to shop from 'mom-and-pop stores', which is retail grocer. Home delivery services, the convenience of being next door, availability of small quantities of goods (like sachets and in low denominations), credit facilities, personalized service etc. are some of the benefits that retain customer loyalty to these outlets.

6. *Kirana* shops are having their own efficient management system and with this they are efficiently fulfilling the needs of the customers. This is one of the good reasons why the customer doesn't want to change their old loyal *kirana* shop.

7. Another reason might be the proximity of the store. It is the convenience store for the customer. In every corner the street an unorganized retail shop can be found that is hardly a walking distance from the customer's house. Many times customers prefer to shop from the nearby kirana shop rather than to drive a long distance organized retail stores.

CONCLUSION

The Indian retail industry comprises of organized and unorganized sectors. Indian retail industry is becoming one of the fastest growing industries in India, especially over the last few years. The India retail industry is expected to grow from Rs. 35,000 crore in 2004-05 to Rs. 109,000 crore by the year 2010, the industry is expected to grow at a pace of 25-30 per cent annually. Organized retail accounts for only 3 per cent participation in total retailing where as rest 97 per cent is captured by the unorganized sector. The development of both the systems simultaneously will definitely boost the competition among retailers, which ultimately give the benefit to the end consumer. Through the growth rate of organized retail is very high, it is facing stiff competition from unorganized retail. Though initially, the retail industry in India was mostly unorganized, however with the change of tastes and preferences of the consumers, the industry is getting more popular these days and getting organized as well. Indian Council for Research on International Economic Relations study said the unorganized retail sector is expected to grow at about 10 per cent per annum with sales rising from $309 billion in 2006-07 to $496 billion in 2011-12. Both sectors are well balanced and their no negative impact of organized retail on unorganized retail sector.

REFERENCES

Kumar, Babita and Gagandeep Banga, Merchandise Planning: An Indispensable Component of Retailing, *ICFAI Journal of Management Research,* Vol. VI, No. 11, 2007.

Chavadi, Chandan A., Shipa S. Kokatnur, Driving Factors and Effectiveness of Sales Promotion in Shopping Malls: A Consumer Prospective, *Indian Journal of Marketing*, April, Volume 40, Page 18.

Kotler, P., Keller K.L., Koshy A., Jha M, (2009) *Marketing Management*, 13th Edition Prentice-Hall, Panchseel Park, New delhi.

Singh, Nityananda (2010) Status of Supply Chain Management in Organized Vs Unorganized Retail, *Indian Journal of Marketing*, March Volume 40, Page 23.

Ramaswami, V.S. and Namkumari, S. (2005) *Marketing Management Planning, Implementation, and Control*, 3rd Edition Macmillan, New Delhi.

Saxena, R. (2009) *Marketing Management*, 4th Edition Tata McGraw-Hill, New Delhi.

Schiffman, L.G. and Kanuk L.L. (2000) *Consumer Behaviour*, 7th Edition Prentice-Hall, Upper Saddler River, New Jersy.

5

Problems and Prospects of Retail Marketing of Agricultural Products

Kabita Kumari Sahu*

Agricultural marketing is a process which starts with a decision to produce a saleable farm product and involves all aspects of market structure or system, both functional and institutional, based on technical and economic consideration. Though agricultural marketing is a State subject, the Government of India has an important role to play in laying down general policy framework, framing of quality standards, conducting survey and research studies and in providing guidance, technical and financial support to the State governments. Agricultural products are mainly sold and purchased through retail markets in India. Agri marketing deals with various aspects of the food supply chain and post production. Approximately 90 per cent of investment in Indian agriculture is production oriented; only 10 per cent is on marketing/post harvest phases. Agri output/agri GDP could get a major fillip due to removal of

* Lecturer in Economics, North Orissa University, Baripada, Orissa.

wastages and reduction of inefficiencies in the agri-marketing process. Post harvest losses account for an estimated 10 per cent of foodgrain production and 25 per cent of fruit and vegetable production. Less than two per cent of fruit and vegetable production is processed. Marketing infrastructure is most important not only for the performance of various marketing functions and for expansion of the size of market but also for transfer of appropriate price signals leading to improved marketing efficiency. The production and marketable surplus of farm produce show that the volume of the commodities to be handled is quite large. The paddy output available for milling per year is around 155 million tonnes. The marketed surplus of cereals is 102.74 million tonnes and pulses is 15.20 million tonnes. Row cotton output is projected to be 3.2 million tonnes per year. The marketable surplus of perishable (fruits vegetables and livestock products) is anticipated to go up 172.69 million tonnes by 2010-11. The capacity to clean grade process store transport etc. to have to expand correspondingly to handle the additional marketed quantities.

In India, the organized marketing of agricultural commodities has been promoted through a network of regulated markets. Most State government and UT administrations have enacted legislations to provide for the regulation of agricultural produce markets. While by the end of 1950, there were 286 regulated markets in the country, their number as on 31 March 2006 stood at 7566. In addition, India has 21,780 rural periodical markets, about 15 per cent of which function under the ambit of regulation. The advent of regulated markets has helped in mitigating the market handicaps of producers/sellers at the wholesale assembling level. But the rural periodic markets in general, and the tribal markets in particular, remained out of its developmental ambit. Indian agricultural production and marketing has set new mile stones in its progress. Tremendous strides have been made in recent past. All time high record of production of 209 million tonnes of food grains in 1999-2000 and 137 million tonnes of fruits and vegetables etc. reminds us of reviewing the past and the strategies to be conceptualized keeping in view the future and fast changing scenario. The increased trend in production has brought in its wake new challenges to handle in terms of huge marketable surplus. A strong and efficient marketing systems is the core content of agricultural marketing in the country keeping in view thee management of marketable surplus. It is also noteworthy to find the markets overseas keeping in view the policy of liberalization.

AGRICULTURAL MARKETING IN INDIA

Government organized marketing of agriculture in the country through the network of regulated markets established under the provisions of the Agricultural Produce Market Act enacted by the States and union territories. As on 31-3-2001 the markets covered under regulation is 7177. In addition there are 27,924 rural periodical markets or hats. About 15 per cent of these in markets have been brought under the ambit of the regulation. The regulated markets have helped in mitigating the market handicaps of producer's sellers. These have also provided physical facilities and institutional environment to the wholesalers commission agents. Traders and other functionaries for conducting activities. It was envisaged that these regulated markets will provide facilities and services which would attract the farmers and buyers creating competitive trade environment thereby offering best of prices to the producer-sellers.

Studies of regulated markets show that they have achieved limited success in providing need based facilities and services conducive to achieving greater marketing efficiency. Most of these markets lack requisite facilities for handling the produce arriving in the yard. Rural markets in general and tribal hats in particular remained out of the ambit of the development. Over a period of time these markets have acquired the status of institution with control and restrictions providing no help in direct marketing organised marketing organised retailing smooth supply of raw material to agro-processing units competitive trading information exchange adoption of innovative marketing system and technologies etc. as was envisaged under the provision of the Act (Chapter on conduct of business powers and duties of the market committee). Monopolistic tendencies and practices have prevented development of free and competitive trade in primary markets future markets (or secondary markets) use of new tools and techniques in pre-harvest management and post-harvest management in handling exports agro-based industries ware housing etc. The prominent activities like grading standardization scientific storage linked with finance search for suitable markets for excess of marketable surplus education of farmers in pre- and post-harvest management and facilities in the markets have become secondary activities. Marketing development funds have been siphoned to public ledger account by the State authorities adversely effecting modernization and infrastructure development vital for operational efficiency. The worldwide Governments have recognized the importance of liberalizing agricultural markets. In South Africa agricultural marketing is changed from controlled marketing to a free system. The ever increasing production spread of latest technologies changing socio-economic environment increasing demand for downsizing the distribution chain reducing the marketing margins between the producers and the ultimate consumers challenges emerging out of liberalization and globalization in the post WTO period required a vibrant dynamic and assimilative marketing structure and system. Food industry plays an important role in retail marketing of agricultural products. The key statistics of of Indian food industry is given Table 5.1.

Table 5.1: Indian Food Industry

Particulars	2002-03	2006-07	2010-11*	2014-15*
Food Industry Size (US $ billion)	175	200	250	300
Food Processing Industry Size (US $ billion)	70	85	110	150
% of food processing in total food industry	40	43	44	50
Organized food processing (US $ billion)	13	23	37	60
% Organized sector in food processing industry	19	27	36	40
Organized Food processing in Food Industry	7.6	11.6	15.8	20

Source: Technopak.

The percentage of food processing in total food industry is increasing from 40 per cent in 2002-03 to 44 per cent in 2010-11. So food processing industry is becoming increasingly important over time.

SINGLE-AGRICULTURAL MARKET

A single unified market does not exist within India and there are significant inter-State barriers to trade. The barriers to single market can broadly be categorized into taxation related barriers and physical barriers as discussed below:

Taxation Related Barriers

1. Variation in rates across states (rationalized after VAT introduction, but not eliminated, leads to evasion through paper trades by unscrupulous players).
2. High rates (most common rate of four per cent appears low, but given the low margins in agri business, this rate is also an incentive for evasion).
3. Multi-point taxation (APMC cess is collected at multiple points; cascading impact on prices.

Physical Barriers

1. Through Essential Commodities Act (physical controls like stock limits at times of short-term shortages lead to long-term supply distortions; restrictions on movement of specific commodities create situation of uncertainty).
2. Through check posts (more serious in case of perishable agri produce).
3. Through APMC regulations (restricts movement of agri produce to attractive.
4. Markets over long distance; restricts ability of farmers to manage price risk).

The private sector has always played a key role in developing marketing infrastructure for agriculture. However, this infrastructure is limited the form of warehousing, cold storage and pack-houses. Provided adequate government support in terms of a conducive policy regime, minimum guarantee of returns (as is the case with other infrastructure such as power and road), fair competition (monopoly of APMC markets), the private sector can play a much bigger role in the area of agricultural marketing and infrastructure development.

SUGGESTIONS FOR IMPROVING AGRICULTURAL MARKETING

In order to have vibrant competitive marketing systems, the Government had to bring about reforms in existing policies rules and regulations with a view to remove all legal provisions inhibiting free marketing system. This is necessary to explore market access opportunities provided by liberalization. Some of the legal provision inhibiting development of vibrant dynamic and assimilative marketing structure and systems is the Agricultural Produce Marketing (Regulation) Act. The Expert Committee on Strengthening and Development of Agricultural Marketing suggested various reforms in the statutory arrangements relating to agricultural marketing as well as policies and programmes for development and strengthening of agricultural Marketing with a specific reference to needed investment package of incentives easy and adequate marketing credit. This committee also recommended a review of the existing legal frame work removal of restrictive provisions to promote competitive marketing structure to promote direct marketing by the farmers to improve price realization to encourage forward and future trading to reduce price risk to induce increase the flow of funds to agricultural sector to support pledge financing by treating it as a direct priority sector lending and to promote market led extension to use of information technology for improving marketing services to the farmers. A inter-ministerial task force under the Chairmanship of Additional Secretary Department of Agriculture and Co-Operation Govt. of India deliberated on these recommendations and identified nine areas. To work out action plan nine inter ministerial sub groups were constituted. The sub-groups on legal-reforms in Agricultural Marketing under the Chairman ship of the Joint Secretary (Marketing). The specific areas identified for reforms in the State Agricultural Produce Marketing Regulations Acts (APMC) are:

Promotion of Integrated Markets in Private/Co-Operative Sector

It is the State government who are alone empowered to initiate the process of setting up a market for certain commodities to be regulated for a defined area, in which regulation is to be enforced under the provision of APMC Act. As a result of this provision the process of initiation of a market the service providers of agricultural marketing do not have any role. Thus, the service providers and/or any other individual or body of individuals can not take initiatives for evaluation of viability and feasibility for setting up of a well developed market with amenities and facilities required at a competitive cost. It is high time that all other States follow suit by amending the APMC Act in their respective states for providing establishment of alternate marketing structures in the shape of 'National Integrated Produce Market' to be owned and managed in the private sector or co-operatives sectors or farmers self help groups farmers associations private entrepreneurs or joint ventures. The service provider may be allowed to levy and collect service charge from the users who may be the producers-sellers or from the market users.The integrated market infrastructure services will in addition to the physical infrastructure include:

1. Assembling
2. Cleaning, Sorting, Grading, packaging and quality certification
3. Storage and finance
4. Transport
5. Retailing and Wholesaling
6. E-trading
7. Warehousing and pledge financing
8. Value addition and
9. Market information exchange service.

Direct Marketing

The direct marketing enables farmers to meet the specific demands of wholesalers or traders from the farmers inventory of graded and certified produce on one hand and of consumers based on consumers preference on the other hand helps the farmers to dynamically take advantage of favourable prices reduce marketing cost and thus their net margins. This encourages farmers to under take cleaning, sorting, grading and quality marking at the farm gate. This will obviate the need to haul the produce to the regulated markets which are not necessarily equipped with all required services and facilities affecting the marketing efficiency adversely. It is reported that the consumers prices declined by the 20 to 30 per cent and producers received the prices rose by 10 to 20 per cent in South Korea as a consequence of expansion of direct marketing of Agricultural Products. Conserted efforts have not been made to promote the direct sales by the farmers to consumers or retailers without involving any intermediary in between. In a country like ours there are large numbers of places where such markets could come up in organised sectors with private investment and can be developed in tuned with the time for forward and backward linkages.

Contract Farming

Contract farming may be defined as an agreement between processing and/or marketing firms for production support at production support at predetermined prices. This stipulates a commitment on the part of the farmers to provide a specific commodity in terms of quality and quantity as determined by the purchaser and commitment on the part of company to support the farmer for production through inputs and other technical support contract farming is becoming popular in recent years and there are number of success stories like Maul, NDDB, PEPSI Co. etc. The Contract farming needs to be further developed after identifying areas commodities and markets for market oriented and demand driven production planning. However while providing for this system of alternate marketing under the APMC Act it is necessary to draft any appropriate legislation separately for ensuring definition of terms and conditions of the agreement keeping in view the objectives.

Direct Contract between Producers and Processing Factories

Presently the farmers are not in position to enter into direct contract with the processors/manufacturers located outside the market area as the commodity has to channels through regulated markets. Or in other words producer is not free to sale his produce by entering in to direct contract without attracting the provisions of this act whether inside or outside the market area. The direct contract between the producers and processing factories or bulk processors will provide monitory gains to the producers through improved competitiveness and the consumers by way of reasonable prices. The provision has to be made through an amendment in the present market act.

Direct Purchase from Farmers Without Any Licence

As per the provisions of the present Act once a market area is notified no person can set up establish or use any place for the purchase sale storage and regiment curing pressing or processing of any agricultural produce or products of livestock or for the purchase or sale of livestock except in accordance with the condition of a license granted by the market committee. This provision prohibits free sale and purchase of agricultural commodities thereby adversely affecting the competitive pricing adds to marketing costs to the produces in the event of bringing the produce to the market yard for improving competitiveness and greater marketing efficiency and pricing edge the producer nay be allowed to sell the produce at the farm gate or threshing floor. This will promote direct contract between the producers and the processing factories with monitory gains to the producers processors and finally to the consumers in the free market.

Notification of Commodities

Under the APM Act the State Government is empowered to notify agricultural Commodities under the provisions of the Act for the purpose of regulation of marketing. This has resulted into anomaly. Even commodities not passing through the market yard or for which no services are provided are also notified. It is logical that only such commodities be notified which pass through the market yard or for which marketing infrastructure has been provided and the market fee should be in proportion to the infrastructure and facilities provided.

Single Point Levy of Market Fee

At present by and large market fee is collected on a particular lot whenever it is transacted. These amounts to multiple point collection simplification of market fee and thus adding to the cost therefore it is necessary to introduce single point levy of market fee in the entire process of marketing in the country.

Tax

There is considerable variation in the structure of taxes and fees on the agricultural produce in various states. This distorts the operation of the domestic market giving wrong signals to the farmers adversely affecting the operational efficiency of the private trade farmer's co-operatives and public sector agencies. It is necessary to bring uniformity in the state level tax structure in agricultural commodities for improving the marketing efficiencies. The ever-increasing marketable surplus will require matching infrastructure and facilities more so in the light of globalization and liberalization. For attracting the private sector investment of this order it is necessary to have proper orientation. This will require:

1. Reducing the regulatory controls and simplifying the procedures;
2. Active stance by the Central Government in some initiatives;
3. Making complementary investment by the State Government and Central Government;
4. Subsidizing a few activities to enable the private sector initiatives to attain viability; and

5. Ensuring adequate credit flow to agricultural marketing activities.

CONCLUSION

Farmers are most vulnerable to marketing related risks such as fluctuation in commodity prices due to their poor holding capacity and cash requirement for the next crop. The government has been trying to implement various market mechanisms to cover farmers' market related risks – future and spot trade of agricultural commodities through electronic exchanges; implementation of warehousing receipt system. However, the real benefits of these instruments have not reached the target beneficiaries due to limited awareness and frequent changes in government policy regarding commodity futures. Despite the realization on the difference that agri marketing can make, little headway has been made over the last decade on account of inherent structural challenges in the Indian agricultural system. These include:

1. lack of implementation of APMC Act;
2. lack of a single unified market;
3. inadequate private investment;
4. few risk mitigation platforms in Indian agriculture. So Investment in agri marketing reforms will be evaluated on risk-return profile;
5. Information and communication technology will play a crucial role; and
6. Development of organized retail in food products has become a necessity for transforming the agri marketing network in India.

There is immense opportunity and increasing role of private players in improving efficiencies in the agri marketing value chain. Promoting private investments in marketing infrastructure will lead to increased efficiency in planning, management and operation of even the existing infrastructure. Avenues for involvement include contract farming, PPP in agri-marketing, direct marketing, and terminal markets among others. It is believed that agri marketing reforms, when implemented, could have significant implications on food processors and retailers through cheaper inputs, stable supply of raw materials and customized produce in terms of quality. This would benefit organized food and grocery retailers and processed food companies.

REFERENCES

Masood, Humayun. and Tabassum, Kaynat (2007): "Indian Agriculture: Problems and Prospects", *Kurukshetra*, July, pp. 19-21.

Mishra, B.N. (1988), "Major Issues in Agricultural Development." *Indian Journal of Agricultural Economics*. November, Vol. XLIII, No. 8.

Singh, Jitedra (2007), "Present Agricultural Scenaria in India", *Kurukshetra*, July, pp. 23-35.

Tripathy, K.K, and Jain, S.K (2007): "Agriculture in the Post Reform Era: Issues, Challenges and Policy Options", *Kurukshetra*, July,. pp. 3-10.

Vaidyanathan, A. and C. Mukherji (1980), Growth and Fluctuation of Food Grains Yields: A State Wise Analysis, *IJAE*, April-June.

6

Emerging Retail Industry for Economic Development

Dibyasingh Gochhayat*
S.S. Nayak**

INTRODUCTION

Retail industry is the world's largest private industry with $ 6.6 trillion turnover and 50 of the top fortune 500 companies and 25 of the top 200 Asians companies being retailers have its revolutionary emergence world over including the East, Middle East and South East. Retail industry is the country's largest source of employment after agriculture. It has the deepest penetration into rural India and generates more than 10 per cent of county's gross domestic product. The Indian retail industry is likely to grow rapidly with shopping malls in large cities and development plan is being projected to establish 150 new shopping malls by 2008.

* Reader in Commerce, Government Autonomous College, Phulbani.

** Lecturer in Commerce, R.N. College, Dura, Berhampur, Ganjam.

OBJECTIVE OF THE STUDY

The Indian retailing market is in a state of inefficiency and it is quite likely that a section of the domestic retailing industry will be severely due to entry of foreign retail industry. To keep pace with foreign retail industry the following factors will taken into consideration:

1. Growth of infrastructure.
2. Inflow of investment and funds.
3. Technical know-how or knowledge base.
4. Reduced cost and increased efficiency.
5. Franchising opportunity for local entrepreneurs.
6. Investments in supply chain, cold chain and warehousing.
7. Implementation of IT in retail industry.
8. Stimulate infant industry and other supporting industry provide better value to and customers.
9. Provide better value to end customers.
10. Relaxation of labour laws, taxes and land-ceiling Acts.

DEVELOPMENT OF RETAIL INDUSTRY IN THE WORLD

In the developed countries, retail industry has developed into a full-fledged industry where more than three-fourths of the total retail trade is done by the organise sector. In India retail giant like Mc Doland, Big Bazar, Subhiksha, Reliance are now replacing the individual small stores. Large retail formats with high quality ambiance and courteous, and well-trained sales staff are regular features of these retailers. Worldwide retail chains like Wal-Mart, Carrefour Group, Sears, K-Mart, McDolands, etc. are considered as major players in organized retail.

The United States of America (U.S.A) has been a pioneer in the evolution of retailing. Today, the organized players handle 80 per cent of the retail trade in the U.S., Wal-Mart alone handles 6 per cent of the total retail trade and the top 50 retailers control 36 per cent of the organized retail. There are following factors that contributed towards the growth of organized in the US:

- Increase in population
- Increased per capita spending
- Dual income families
- Urbanization
- Covering distances has become easier

Table 6.1: Top Ten Retailers of World

Rank	Retailer	No. of stores owned	Annual Sales (in US $ Millions)
1.	Wall-Mart Stores Inc. (USA)	4178	$180,787
2.	Carrefour Group (France)	8130	$61,047
3.	The Froger Co. (USA)	3445	$49,000
4.	The Home Depot, Inc. (USA)	1134	$45,738
5.	Royal Anold (Netherlands)	7150	$45,729
6.	Metro AG (Germany)	2169	$44,189
7.	Kmart Corporation (USA)	2105	$37,028
8.	Sears, Roebuck and Co. (USA)	2231	$36,823
9.	Albertson's, Inc. (USA)	2512	$36,726
10.	Target Corporation (USA)	1307	$36,362

Development of retail industry in India is the country having the most unorganized retail market. In India, things started to change slowly in the 1980s, when India first began opening its economy. Textiles sector (which companies like Bombay Dyeing, Raymond, S.Kumar and Grasim was the first to see the emergence of retail chains. Later on, Titan, maker of premium watches, successfully created an organized retailing concept in India by establishing a series of elegant showrooms.

Table 6.2: Nationwide Top Ten Retailers

Retailer	Current Format	New Formats Experimenting with
Shopper's Stop	Department Store	Quasi-mail
Ebony	Department Store	Quasi-mail, smaller outlets, adding food retail
Crossword	Large bookstore	Corner shops
Piramyd	Department Store	Quasi-mail, food retail
Pantaloon	Own brand store	Hypermarket
Subhiksha	Supermarket	Considering moving to self service
Vitan	Supermarket	Sub-urban discount store
Food world	Food Supermarket	Hypermarket food world express
Globus	Department Store	Small fashion stores
Big Bazar	Supermarket	Considering moving to self service

The Indian retail sector is estimated at around Rs. 900,000 crore, of which the organized sector accounts for a mere two per cent indicating a vast potential market opportunity that is waiting for the consumer-savvy organized retailer.

CHALLENGES

1. **Global Challenges:** The Indian retail sector is facing the challenges by the influx of global retail players like Wal-mart, Carrefour, Sears, K.Mart and McDonalds. They have a better understanding of the Indian consumer's mind.

2. **Industry Challenges:** Retail, a multi-trillion dollar Industry across the world faces a plethora of problems

due to intense competition, customer acquisition and retention, supply chain management and automation, IT infrastructure and workforce management. They can be addressed with the right technology that identifies the problems and offers a holistic solution.

3. **Customer Service:** Multinational corporations treat their customers as king. They try to satisfy their customers by dint of qualitative product at reasonable price. A dissatisfied customer will never repeat the business within the organisation.

4. **Multi-sales Channels Availability:** With the changing business scenario consumers are finding it easy to get the best prices on the internet without going to nearest stores and spend hours together. As a result footfalls are decreasing in retail stores. And retailers who do not provide additional channels for customers are taking a hit.

5. **Increase Competition:** Due to increase computation consumers are desiring for best deals often via web or through the manufactures; the retail sector is struggling to sustain and grow due to wafer thin margin and competitors are offering special gifts and discounts to capture them.

6. **Communication Infrastructure Improvement:** Communication infrastructure should be developed to contact the existing as well as prospective customers.

OPPORTUNITIES

1. **Benefit to Unemployed Youth:** Retail sector is the country's largest source of employment after agriculture. It provides employment to unemployed youth. This sector is expected to create 2.5 million jobs by 2010. Twenty crore people are dependent on this sector. In software field attractive salary packages are being paid to attract the youth more and more.

2. **Benefit to Retailer:** Retailers are able to sell their goods directly to the ultimate consumers. This saves from long channel of distribution.

3. **Benefit to Overall Economy:** According to a study it has been found that retailing contributes more than 10 per cent of G.D.P. India is the fourth largest economy as regards G.D.P.

4. **Benefit to Consumers:**
   (a) Quality product
   (b) Reasonable price due to stiff competition
   (c) Business groups are trying to establish super market, hyper market and shopping malls to bring revolution in retail industry.

5. **Other Benefits:**
   (a) Growth of infrastructure
   (b) Inflow of investment and funds
   (c) Reduced cost and increased efficiency
   (d) Implementation of IT in retail
   (e) Stimulate infant industry and other supporting industry
   (f) Technical know-how
   (g) Franchising opportunity for local entrepreneur
   (h) Investment in supply chain, cold chain and warehousing
   (i) Increased number and improved quality of employment
   (j) Increased local sourcing

CONCLUSION

In the developed country's, the retail industry has developed into a full-fledged Industry where more than three-fourths of the total retail trade is done by the organised sector. In India the country is having the most unorganised retail market. In India things started to change slowly in the 1980s, when India first began opening its economy. Textiles sector like Bombay Dyeing, Raymond, S.Kumar and Grasim was the first to see the emergence of retail chains. Later on Titan, maker of premium watches successfully created an organised retailing concept in India by establishing a series elegant showrooms. The United States of America (U.S.A.) has been a pioneer in the evolution of retailing. Today the organised players handle 80 per cent of the retail trade in U.S. Walmart alone handles six per cent of the retail trade in U.S.A. Retail Industry is the largest source of employment after agriculture and generates more than 10 per cent of country's gross domestic product.

REFERENCES

William J.Stanton, Bruce J.Walket, *Fundamentals of Marketing*, Mc GrawHill, Inc. 1994.

Michael J.Etzel, *Handbook of Retailing*, ICFAI, Berhampur, 2008.

V.S.Rama Swamy & S.Namakumari, *Marketing Management, Planning Implementation & Control*, Macmillan Business Books, 2004.

Kotler, Philip, *Marketing Management, The Millennium Edition*, 'Prentice-Hall of India Pvt. Ltd., New Delhi, 1999.

4PS Business and Marketing, February 01-14-2008.

7

Attitude and Preference of Customer Towards Buying Fast Moving Consumer Goods (FMCGs) in Puducherry

R. Srinivasan*

ABSTRACT

We fit into place in some form, just about every moment of our lives. When we watch an advertisement on TV, talk to friends about a movie just saw, brush our teeth, buy a new TV, throw away an old pair of shoes, complain to a store about the poor quality of an item we just bought, exchange our shopping experience in the store recently visited by us, we are behaving as a consumer.

Given its omnipresence, the article on consumer behaviour can be fascinating. This article is an endeavour to analyze:

- Why we buy from a certain store type?

* Associate Professor, PG & Research Department of Corporate Secretaryship, Bharatidarshan Government College for Women (Autonomous), Puduchery.

- What are the factors which influence our decision on store type?
- What are the changing potentials of the consumer towards future store choice?

This topic is highly relevant in the present retail marketing scenario for FMCG as we see that globalization will be the defining force in the FMCG sector in the next decade. In continuation of the above passages, it is found that, India is on a buying extravaganza and so are the residents of Puducherry. The shopping malls, supermarkets, hypermarkets have today become the prime drivers of the organized retail revolution in the country. Over the past five years, people in the metros are under the spell of the mall culture. Shopping has been revolutionized with the arrival of malls and the new generation Indian consumer has not only shifted to the modern format "experiential store" but is also ready for a truly international shopping experience. According to KSA Techno Pak study there were just three malls in India in the year 2000. By the year 2007, the figure is expected to cross 343. A significant number of new and small malls will be located in small towns like Tier 2 cities of Bhopal, Baroda, Coimbatore, Puducherry etc. It is highly relevant in today's context as we see that retail sector is the sunrise industry of our country. It is the largest private sector industry contributing towards the economic prosperity of our country. Further, at this time corporate are looking at the rural and semi-urban areas to fill their cash registers, as the consumers in these areas are also increasingly becoming brand conscious and show changing lifestyle patterns. Further it is also observed that trade, media and FMCG would be active hiring sectors in the current quarter of the year 2007-08. According to the third quarterly employment outlook released by Team Lease Services Pvt. Ltd., net employment outlook in these three sectors (86 points) will be the highest in the quarter April-June 2007. Also business confidence looks positive with a boom in the retail sector taking centre stage. This study hence becomes more significant, as it is conducted in Puducherry town.

INTRODUCTION

Puducherry is a complete town with its mix of Indian and French culture. The town has a serene atmosphere and faces the Bay of Bengal on the East Coast Road. It is a growing tourist destination for the domestic and International tourists. The increasing disposable incomes, changing spending habits, consumption patterns and leisure time are laying foundation to the organized retail industry for fast moving consumer goods here in the Puducherry. The small town already has large super markets like Nilgiris, Spencers Daily, Amudhasurabi, Subhiksha, Oviya, Devi Super Shoppe also including large number of discount stores, departmental stores and convenience stores competition with the organized retailers. Now Reliance is also going to set up its Reliance Fresh chain in the town.

This study on the consumer attitude towards retail marketing choice for FMCGs will enable the growing retailers to understand the shopper preferences and attitude in their choice of retail stores for purchase of consumer goods. This will enable to understand the footfalls profile visiting the various retail stores and also answer to questions like what is the major driving force in their choice and their shopping attitude.

The study will help the new organized retail entrants to understand the shopping attitude of the Puducherrians and take competitive measures to win their loyalty. On the other hand it will also help the traditional trade channels to prepare strategies to maintain and increase their consumer loyalty. Hence we can also analyze whether organized retail in FMCG will be a threat to unorganized retail. In this context, An attempt has been made to study the following objectives:

- To study attitude of the residents towards retail choice for FMCG.
- To analyze the perception of the consumers with regard to demographic factors like age, income group, marital status gender etc towards store choice for FMCG.

- To find out the prevailing trends of consumer attitude in terms of:
  - Frequency of their purchase in a preferred store.
  - Major factor influencing them to purchase in a preferred store.
  - Frequency of their visits to different types of retail stores.
  - The extent of store switching among the residents.
  - Ranking of their preferences among retail stores for purchase of monthly groceries.
  - Ranking of the marketing mix factors which is the basis of their store choice.
  - Ranking of the in-store factors which is the basis of their store choice.
  - Preference to purchase branded (Vs) generic products.
- To study the extent of group or individual shopping patterns in the different types of stores.
- To determine the importance given to traveling distance in store choice.
- To study the post purchase satisfaction level of the customer in the different type of retail stores of their choice.
- To determine their opinion on inducement shopping in terms of retail stores.
- To study their preferred level of service, time, day preference.

To understand the preference of the respondents to the various ancillary services offered by the growing retailers to provide overall shopping experience in the retail store.

The focus of the article is to analyze the shopping attitude of the consumers of different demographic profile in terms of:

- What type of retail store they prefer?
- What is the major factor influencing the retail choice?
- What are the consumer shopping friends observed in retail choice.
- To what extent they show store switching patterns etc.

A questionnaire was designed and developed to collect information on the attitudes of the consumers in retail store choice for FMCGs. It was debugged and pilot tested on a sample of 6 respondents. The questionnaire was a structured questionnaire and consisted of two sections dealing with:

- Demographic profile of the consumers
- Shopping attitude of the consumers.

The responses elicited for the pilot study were similar and drawn from the same population. Some changes were made to the first version of the questionnaire, including removal and addition of some items to make the questionnaire shorter and more reliable. The standardized questionnaire was then used for the survey.

The secondary sources referred for the study are as follows: books, websites magazines, journals, newspapers etc.

Following three sampling decisions were made with respect to the study:

1. **Sampling Unit:** Who is to be surveyed? The target respondents' were residents in the town of Puducherry who are the potential customers' visiting the various types of retail stores considered for the project under study. Respondents belonging to different demographic profiles were chosen for the survey.
2. **Sample Size:** The sample size decided for the study was 100 respondents.
3. **Sampling Procedure:** Non-probability sample technique namely convenience sampling was chosen. That is accessible target population members were selected for the study.

SAMPLE AREA OF THE STUDY

The area of the study was the union territory of Puducherry.

STATISTICALS TOOLS USED

The study uses statistical tools like percentage analysis, ranking method, opinion rating scales, Likert summated rating scale, Chi-square test, Anova (two way analysis of variance) Yules coefficient of of association, Bar charts and pie diagrams.

YULES COEFFICIENT OF ASSOCIATION

The most popular method of studying association is the yules coefficient because here not only we can determine the nature of association i.e whether the attributes are positively associated, negatively associated or independent, but also the degree or extent to which the two attributes are associated. The coefficient is denoted by the symbol Q and is obtained by applying the following formula:

$$Q = \frac{(AB)(\propto\beta)-(A\beta)(\propto\beta)}{(AB)(\propto\beta)+(A\beta)(\propto\beta)}$$

The value of this coefficient lies between $\pm$ 1. When it is +1 it is perfectly positive and when it is -1 it is perfect negative association. When Q is O the two variables are independent.

CHI-SQUARE TEST

This is one of the simplest and most widely used non-parametric tests in statistical work. The symbol χ^2 is a Greek letter chi.

It is defined as:

$$\frac{\sum(O-E)^2}{E}$$

where O refers to the observed frequencies and E refers to the expected frequencies.

STEPS IN CHI SQUARE

1. Expected frequency is calculated

$$E = \frac{ET \times CT}{N}$$

E = Expected frequency

RT = Row total for the row containing the cell

CT = Column total for the column containing the cell

N = Total number of observations

2. Then (O-E) is calculated and $(O-E)^2$ is determined.
3. Then $(O-E)^2/E$ is calculated for each frequency.
4. Then summation of $(O-E)^2/E$ for all frequencies is calculated.

If the calculated value is greater than the table value then the null hypothesis proposed is rejected. Hypothesis proposed for the study were tested using this method.

In order to accomplish the objectives set out for this research, responses were classified according to their personal profile with the help of frequency tables. Statistical tools such as percentage analysis, comparative analysis using five point scaling technique, mean method and rank correlation, chi square test, Yule's coefficient of association, ANOVA was used for testing of the hypothesis.

Utmost care and efforts have been taken by the researcher to avoid errors, faults, shortcomings in the process of data collection. In spite of that, this study is prone to some limitations which are mentioned below:

1. This study considers the consumer attitude towards retail marketing in the purchase of FMCGs only.

2. The sample size is limited to 100 respondents.
3. Student samples were also used in the stud, despite the criticism that they might be atypical consumers because of their restricted age range, limited consumption experience and relatively low income.
4. This study uses a market level aggregate model to understand consumer attitude towards retail marketing choice for FMCGs.
5. Lengthy questionnaire was used to collect the needed data. This may have the chances of inclusion of bias in the data collected.
6. This study is limited only to the town of Puducherry and hence generalization cannot be made.
7. There may be bias due to the data collection instrument used. Questionnaire when given to respondents, they may have either rated on the higher or lower side. This error is more when rating scales are used.
8. The sample size of 50+age group is also limited. This is the growing generation whose spending power is also increasing unlike in the past.
9. The tools used in the study has its own limitations.

INDIAN CORPORATES VENTURING INTO RETAILING

- The Mukesh Ambani headed Reliance Group has ventured into Retail Supermarket Chains by launching Reliance Fresh stores. The first test market stores of Reliance Fresh was launched in Banjara Hills in Hyderabad in January 2007. The company has also started to establish its Reliance Fresh stores in major metros and other important cities in its Phase I of this Project.
- The A.V. Birla Group has taken over Trinethra Super Retail Ltd. of Andhra Pradesh, which has about 100 retail outlets in south India. With this A.V. Birla Group is also entering into the Retail Supermarket Competition (News released On January 2007).

- Bharathi Group headed by Sunil Mittal has tied up with the global giant in Retail Supermarket, Wal-Mart after a lot of controversy and opposition from the local small traders in groceries, fruits and vegetables. This group plans investment of 2.5 billion dollars in the retail venture by 2015. This investment will be made in hypermarkets, supermarkets chains in our country.
- The Indian economy spinner TATA group is in talks with another global giant in retail, Woolworths. Woolworths would be their preferred retail partner for its foray in the future for food and grocery retailing.
- Retail chain Nilgris Dairy farm has drawn up an aggressive growth plan for its own brand products in bakery, dairy and foods. The new management team of Nilgris headed by Managing Directors Mr. N.C. Venugopal and Chairman Mr. Raja Chellayan, has drawn up a plan entailing Rs. 120 cores of investment to increase its store strength to 500 from the present 40 stores by 2010.
- **Subhiksha** - Its goal is to become India's favourite neighbourhood store. It aims at becoming a 1000 store retail chain in India. As on 13th December 2006 the company launched its retail outlets in Maharashtra and completed its 600 stores target in its Phase I Project.

Thus we see a number of our Indian corporates entering into the nascent retail sector business in our country. This again makes this study very important for the retailing corporations, to understand shopper behaviour and develop new strategies to influence consumers at the point of purchase.

Table 7.1 shows the list of studies that were referred for the article from publications in major scholarly journals and magazines.

Table 7.1: List of Studies Preferred for this Article

Sl. No.	Author/s	Study Objective/Title	Seminar/Research Origin/Publication Name and Year
1	2	3	4
1.	Wharton Marketing Professor Eric Brad Low and Doctoral student Sam Hui	The traveling salesman goes grocery shopping: The systematic inefficiencies of grocery paths.	Research paper, 2006
2.	Rajiv Banerjee Editor at Times group	A few good men	Brand equity, ET, 2007.
3.	Bindu D. Menon editor at Times group	The retail rollover	Brand equity, ET, 2007
4.	Ravi Pappu, senior lecturer Pascale Quester, professor at University of Queensland Business School, Australia	Does customer satisfaction lead to improved brand equity - an empirical examination of two categories of retail brands.	The ICFAI journal of brand management, 2007.
5.	Sandhya Mehta	Upcoming malls – shoppers paradise?	The ICFAI university press, Marketing Mastermind, 2006.
6.	Tim Morris senior researcher	Retail supermarket globalisation whose winning?	Cariolis research group analysis, 2001.

(Contd...)

1	2	3	4
7.	Ashley Coutinho	Shop, skip and jump	Brand equity, ET, 2007.
8.	Anand Ramanathan & Manu Parashar – research scholar IIM, Bangalore.	A typology of format adaptation strategies in comparative retailing.	Research paper from IIM, Bangalore.
9.	Dr. (Ms.) Carol Cosgrove sacks director UNECE.	Access to international supply chains in developed markets.	Paper presentation at Asian Seminar on Safe and High Quality Food for International Trade, New Delhi, 2002.
10.	Dave. D Weather Spoon and Thomas Reardon research scholars at Michigan State University, USA.	A study on the rise of supermarkets in Africa	Research paper in 2006 at Michigan State University
11.	Pappu R. Quester & Cooksey RW University of Queensland Business School, Australia.	Consumer-based brand equity: Improving the measurement – empirical evidence.	Journal of Product and Brand Management, 2005.
12.	Cundiff Edward	Concepts in comparative retailing.	Journal of Marketing, 1995.
13.	Goldman Arieh	The transfer of retail formats into developing countries: The example of China.	Journal of retailing, 2001.
			(Contd…)

1	2	3	4
14.	D. Majumdar Senior researcher in a Japanese MNC.	FDI in retailing: India as a supermarket.	*Business Standard*, 2007.
15.	Report submitted by ICICI Bank	Foreign direct investment in retail.	Study report published by ICICI, 2004.
16.	Bloemer J and Odekesken Schroder G.	Store satisfaction and store loyalty explained by customer and store related factors.	Journal of Consumer Satisfaction, Dissatisfaction and Complaining Attitude, 2002.
17.	Feuer. J research scholar	Retailing grows up, looks to image-building.	*Ad Week*, 2005.
18.	J. Padmapriya	Shopping Mania	Brand equity, ET, 2007.
19.	Vikash & Bharathy Tamilan Editors	The meeting of the extremes	*Nanayam*, 1-15 April 2007
20.	Nanthini Dominique Editor, The Hindu	The Brand Conscious Puducherian	*The Hindu*, March 24, 2007

ANALYSIS

This article attempts to provide a comparative analysis of the data collected for the research work with the help of statistical tools and techniques. Table 7.2 shows the frequency of purchase exhibited by the respondents in the major types of retail stores.

Table 7.2: Frequency of Purchase in the Different Types of Retail Stores

Retail Stores	Frequency of Purchase				Total
	Daily	Weekly	Fortnightly	Monthly	
Supermarket	–	15	1	13	29
Departmental Store	–	5	3	5	13
Discount Store	1	10	3	9	23
Convenience Store	13	15	1	6	36
Total	**14**	**45**	**8**	**33**	**100**

Source: Primary Data.

The above table are coded by subtracting from each figure the value 6. The data in the coded form are shown in Table 7.3.

STATISTICAL TEST

Analysis of variance (Two way)

PROPOSED HYPOTHESES

1. Does consumer preference for stores differ significantly?
2. Is there any significant difference in the frequencies of purchase pattern exhibited by the consumers in the four major types of retail stores?

Let us take the hypothesis; there is no difference between the frequencies of purchase pattern among the four types of retail stores.

Table value of F for $v_1 = 3$ and $V_2 = 9 = 8.8123$

Table 7.3: Data in Coded Form

Retail Stores	Frequency of Purchase				Total
	Daily	Weekly	Fortnight	Monthly	
Supermarket	-6	9	-5	7	5
Departmental Store	-6	-1	-3	-1	-11
Discount Store	-5	4	-3	3	-1
Convenience Store	7	9	-5	0	11
Total	**-10**	**21**	**-16**	**9**	**4**

Source: Primary Data.

SOURCES OF VARIATION

Table 7.4: Sources of Variation

Sources of Variation	Sum of Squares	V	Means Squares
Between frequencies	218.6	3	72.87
Between Stores	66.2	3	22.01
Residual	167.2	9	18.58
Total	**452**	**15**	

The calculated value (3.92) is less than table value and we conclude that there is no difference in the frequencies of purchase.

Now let us compare store variance with residual variance

$$F = \frac{22.01}{18.58} = 1.18$$

Table value of F at (3, 9) = 8.8123 hence there is no significant difference in the store preference among the respondents.

Table 7.5 shows the level of importance given to the travelling distance by different income groups as a factor influencing the choice of retail store type by the respondents.

Table 7.5: Income Group and Travelling Distance Importance Level

Importance Level	≤ 15000	15000 +	Total Respondents
Important	15	27	42
Very Important	19	18	37
Not Important	15	6	21
Total	**49**	**51**	**100**

Chi-Square Test

Proposed Hypothesis

H_0: There is no association between income group and importance level given by them to the travelling distance in retail store choice.

Table 7.6: Applying Chi Square test

O	E	$(O-E)^2$	$(O-E)^2/E$
15	20.58	31.14	2.08
27	24.42	31.14	1.19
19	18.13	0.76	0.04
18	18.87	0.76	0.04
15	10.29	22.18	1.48
6	10.71	22.18	3.70

Source: Primary Data.

Table value of χ^2 for degree of freedom V = 2, and 5% level of significance is 5.99.Since the calculated value of Chi-square is greater than the table value of Chi-square the above null hypothesis is rejected and we conclude that there is an association between income group and their level of importance given to travelling distance in retail store choice among the respondents.

Table 7.7 shows the type of retail store preferred by the respondents in the two age groups ≤ 30 and 30+ among the respondents.

Table 7.7: Age Group Vs. Retail Store Choice for FMCGs

Age Group	Type of Retail Store		% of Respondents
	Organized	Unorganized	
≤ 30	17	11	28
30+	34	38	72
Total	**51**	**49**	**100**

Source: Primary Data.

Applying Yule's Coefficient of Association from the above table, we get

$AB = 17 \quad A\beta = 34$

$\propto B = 11 \quad \propto\beta = 38$

Yule's coefficient of association

$$Q = \frac{(AB)(\propto b) - (Ab)(\propto B)}{(AB)(\propto b) + (Ab)(\propto B)}$$

$Q = 0.27$

Thus, we can conclude that there is very low degree of positive association between age group and the type of retail store preferred.

Table 7.8: Income Group Vs. Retail Store Choice for FMCG's

Income Group	Type of Retail Store		Total
	Organized	Unorganized	
≤ 15000	26	40	66
15000 +	25	9	34
Total	**51**	**49**	**100**

Source: Primary Data.

Table 7.8 shows the type of retail store preferred by the respondents in the two income groups ≤ 15000 and 15000 + among the respondents.

Applying Yule's Coefficient of Association from the Table 7.8 can be expressed in terms of these symbols as

$(AB) = 26 \quad (A\beta) = 25$

$(\alpha B) = 40 \quad (\alpha\beta) = 9$

$Q = -0.62$

Thus we can conclude that there is a moderate degree of negative association income group and type of retail store preferred.

Table 7.9 shows the number of the respondents who will wait in their preferred store during rush hours according to their marital status.

Table 7.9: Marital Status and Willingness to Wait during Rush Hours

Status	Wait	Not Wait	% of Respondent
Married	70	8	78
Unmarried	17	5	22
Total	**87**	**13**	**100**

CHI SQUARE TEST (X^2)

H_0: There is no association between marital status of the respondents and their willingness to wait in their preferred store during rush hours.

Since the calculated value of χ^2 is lesser than the table value of χ^2 at 5 per cent level of significance the above null hypothesis is accepted and hence we conclude that there is no association between marital status and their willingness to wait during rush hours.

The expected frequencies shall be calculated as follows Table 7.10.

Table 7.10: Applying Chi-square Test

O	E	O-E	$(O-E)^2$	$(O-E)^2/E$
70	68	2	4	0.059
8	10	-2	4	0.400
17	19	2	4	0.211
5	3	2	4	1.333
Total			$(O - E)^2/E$	**2.003**

Degree of freedom (V) = (2 – 1) (2 – 1) = 1

for V = 1 χ^2 at 5% level of significance = 3.84.

FINDINGS OF THE STUDY

The study on the consumer attitude towards retail marketing choice for FMCGs in the town of Puducherry revealed the following:

- The survey studied the shopping behaviour of respondents in different age and income groups.
- Out of 100 respondents surveyed most of their occupational group was government employees, businesspeople and teachers. The survey also covered to considerable extent homemakers, sales executives, employees in the private sector etc.
- Seventy-eight per cent of the respondents were married and 70 per cent of the respondents were males.
- The preferred supermarket in the town of Puducherry is Nilgris followed by Vijaya Ganapathy Stores.
- The preferred discount stores in the town were Amudhasurabi followed by PAPSCO.
- The preferred department stores in the town is Panduranga stores, Raja stores while, the most favoured convenience store is store located in their neighbourhood.

- The survey revealed that 35 per cent of the respondents regular choice of retail store was convenience store, 29 per cent visited supermarket, 23 per cent visited discount store and 13 per cent visited departmental stores. Thus a majority of the respondents regular choice is close between convenience store and supermarket though convenience store is majorities choice.
- As far as frequency of purchasing is concerned, the respondents preferred store is 45 per cent of them shop weekly followed by 33 per cent of them shopped monthly and about 14 per cent of them shopped daily.
- Purchasing in their preferred store is weekly and 45 per cent of people are inclined.
- It is also observed that weekly and daily purchase frequency is seen with convenience store customers, while monthly or weekly purchase frequency is seen in supermarkets, discount and department stores.
- Fourty-nine per cent of the respondents said that they shopped in a particular store due to quality consideration while 22 per cent gave consideration to the price factor, about 14 per cent for product variety and 12 per cent for service. This shows quality goods is an indispensable factor for store choice.
- It is found that the extent of store loyalty exhibited by the consumers is about 67 per cent only in retail choice for FMCG. This shows that any dissatisfaction experienced by the consumers with respect to there factors will cause them to switch stores. This can also be leveraged upon by the competitors.
- Overall ranking of the respondents preference for retail stores shows rank 1 for convenience followed by an equal position for supermarket and discount store and the last rank for department stores.

- The overall ranking of the marketing mix factors which plays an important role in the consumer retail choice showed that Price is the first major factor followed by place of the store, quality, promotion, product variety, product assortment and lastly delivery of goods. Hence we see that consumers are highly price sensitive in store choice and also give preference to the quality of the products and accessibility to the stores.
- The study on the In-Store factors influencing retail store choice shows that majority of the respondents prefer the self-service facility in choosing a retail store very closely followed by the requirement of friendly salespersons at the store. While shopping experience is only ranked last. it shows that consumers prefer the touch-feel-compare process in store choice.
- Fourty-two per cent of the respondents feel advertisement also influence in retail store choice and about 36 per cent of them are influenced by recommendation of friends and relatives. The sales promotion and brand image of a store has minimum impact only.
- About 62 per cent of the respondents prefer group shopping to individual shopping while choosing retail store for FMCG's. This shows shopping is seen more as an entertainment or leisure activity among the residents.
- About 79 per cent feel that travelling distance to the store does influence the choice of the store. Further, as convenience stores are more early accessible than supermarkets and other stores, hence we see many respondents favoring this store.
- With respect to the respondents level of satisfaction in their preferred stores post purchase service like product returns, money back offers a vast majority are highly satisfied with their stores service. In this perspective there is no significant between the different types of stores.

- About 50 per cent of the respondents feel that inducement shopping is high in supermarket and only about 24 per cent feel it is high in the convenience stores. This is also a major cause for respondents to choose convenience stores.
- However, it is observed that today's respondents are highly self-regulated in the shopping behaviour. Despite the impulse shopping patterns being high in a particular store, they do not take it as criterion in store choice.
- Overall 63 per cent of the respondents prefer self service when compared to limited and full service facilities.
- About 61 per cent of the respondents prefer to shop in the evening, 33 per cent prefer to shop in the moving and only 6 per cent prefer to shop in the afternoon. This shows peak shopping time is evening.
- The preferred day of purchase seems to be monthly and weekends or beginning of the month.
- Applying Spearman's rank correlation cofficient, it has been found that there is a high and direct correlation between respondents regular choice and preferred store choice in the case of purchase of FMCGs. That is respondents are executing their preference towards retail store choice to a large extent.
- An over whelming 91 per cent of the respondents prefer branded to generic items in the stores irrespective of the customers of the different types of retail stores.
- Opinion of the respondents to the upcoming facilities in retail stores reveals that cheque cashing facility followed by credit, parking facility is highly favoured. While provision of rest rooms is least preferred.
- A cross tabulation analysis of the demographic data with the shopping pattern shows that:

    1. Irrespective of age group the choice of retail stores is the same.

2. In the case of income groups the higher income group prefers supermarket and the lower income group prefers convenience stores.

SUGGESTIONS

Though it appears that there is close competition between the organized and the unorganized retail stores in the town of Puducherry. The competition is very strong between supermarkets and convenience stores even though the convenience store is preferred by a maximum number of the respondents. The survey however shows the growing preference for organized retailing due to factors like increasing disposable incomes, increasing leisure time and increasing group shopping habits among the residents. The following suggestions have been put forward for the two major categories of retailers.

For the Organised Retail Marketing (This includes Supermarkets, Discounts Stores, and Shopping malls)

Speciality Stores to Win Competition

Since a number of supermarket chains are focusing attention on the tier II cities & towns. These players should set up some theme or specialty stores. This will give them a competitive advantage.

GOOD CRM *Practices to be enforced*

The survey shows that among the In-store factors self-service and friendly sales persons is the most highly preferred factors. The sales personnel must be properly trained to understand the needs of the customer. They should help the customer only when needed and not be intrusive. Further the customer should not be given the impression of being very closely guarded inside the store.

Reduce Queue at Billing Counters

Most of the respondents say that the waiting time at billing counters is too long. Hence, more number of cash counters should be opened to avoid chaos and confusion. Further separate counters for cash and credit/debit card facilities must be provided to increase the speed of the billing process.

WIDE Coverage of the Markets by the Outlets Required

Retail chain owners should see that at least two franchisee stores of their brands are established. This should be located such that coverage of the market is achieved. This will also help them to win the customers from the other unorganized retail stores in the town. Good parking facilities must be provided at the retail stores.

ATTRACT Customers during off peak purchase hours

Offering of discounts on purchase during off peak time and days can be adopted by stores. This will also avoid rush during peak hours/day. Also during leisure shopping consumers will purchase more variety of the store products.

MAINTAIN GENUINE PRICES and Offer Valid Discounts

Prices of the products should be genuine as price is a major variable influencing store choice. Discounts offered should be valid for a certain period. This will influence the brand image of the company.

Conduct Sales Promotional Activities

- Increase frequency of visit to the stores by conducting theme festivals like cookery festival, children carnivals, vegetables and fruits mela, diet foods mela etc. This can also be conducted on weekdays to avoid traffic.
- Greet your regular customers

During the regular customers birthday, anniversaries send a card to them.

- Provide Ancillary Services to Delight Customers. These services can include trained first aid personnel:

- Kid Zone;
- Baby attendant facility;
- Wash rooms and toilets; and
- Food joints etc.

Thus upcoming retailers to the town of Puducherry can use these suggestions to obtain a competitive advantage over the others.

For the Unorganised Retail Sector

The town of Puducherry being a traditional town, there is a high patronage for the traditional stores to purchase FMCGs. However, with the growing awareness level, leisure time and disposable incomes might cause their customers to switch as the consumers show only a considerable amount of loyalty to their stores. The following measures can be adopted by the retail stores in the unorganized rector:

Take steps to Face Nascent Competition

The organized retail revolution has begun in the town and it is in the nascent state. But the convenience store owners should not relax that they are preferred the most by the consumers. Changing lifestyle is in on the high and so also store loyalty is only up to 67 per cent which is only a moderate percentage.

Give Face Lift for the Stores

Though they are the neighborhood stores . They should also pay attention to better displays, slightly provide facilities for self service if possible to beat their bigger counterparts.

Better Customer Service should be provided by:

1. Updating their inventory and avoid no stock conditions.
2. Obtain access to latest products and place them on the store shelf.

3. Also keep on their store shelf premium and branded products to attract their users.
4. Offer quality packaging for their In-Store products.
5. Provide proper storage facilities to increase the shelf life of the stock and maintain its quality.
6. Quick delivery of goods and through phone calls also. These would enable them to keep their customers with themselves and also attract new ones.

CONCLUSION

A demographic profile analysis of the shopping patterns tells that variables like age group, marital status, occupational group does not significantly influence store choice, while income group has a low moderate degree of influence on the store choice, i.e higher income group prefer organized retail to unorganized retail. But this is only moderate in significance. Consumers have also realized the extent of impulse shopping in a type of retail store but they are of view that they are on their guard towards impulse shopping.

An analysis of the influence of the marketing mix factors on retail store choice revealed that shoppers are highly price sensitive, quality conscious, convenience to shop sensitive while discounts or promotions is not a major consideration when compared to other marketing mix factors.

On an analysis of their in store shopper attitude/ requirements, it is seen that self service is highly preferred by them. This is largely due to the changing lifestyle of the consumers in the town. This shows that consumers give more preference for touch feel-compare process in store choice.

The study shows that the consumers store loyalty is only moderate when it was evaluated using a number of store switching and store sticking attitude. This also shows that if consumers are not satisfied with a stores service level they will switch. Hence, retail stores should ensure high level of satisfaction with the positive factors influencing store choice and vice versa for the negative factors influencing store choice. Further more we also see that today's consumers are well aware and take wise decisions. Overall based on the research data and the literature survey it is seen that in India there is a changing consumer lifestyle characterized by greater per capita income and increasing disposable income. While in specific in Puducherry town it is observed that the residents are increasingly becoming brand conscious, further the nascent retail marketing in the town is gaining momentum to beat the unorganized sectors with their better inventory chain management.

REFERENCES

Arieh, Goldman (2001), "The Transfer of Retail Formats into Developing Countries: The Example of China", *Journal of Retailing*, 2001.

Banerjee, Rajeev (2007), "A Few Good Men", *Brand Equity, Economic Times*, 14 February 2007.

Bindu, D. Menon (2007), "The Retail Rollover", *Brand Equity*, Economic Times.

Bloemer, J and Odekerken RW (2002) "Store Satisfaction and Store Loyalty Explained by Customer and Store Related Factors", *Journal of Consumer Satisfaction, Dissatisfaction and Complaining Attitude*, Vol 15, pp. 68-80.

Bradlow, Eric and Sam Hai RW (2006), "The Travelling Salesman goes Grocery Shopping: The Systematic Inefficiencies of Grocery Paths", 2006.

Cosgrove, Dr. (MS) Carol (2002), "Access to International Supply Chains in Developed Markets" Asian Seminar on Safe and High Quality Food for International Trade, New Delhi, 2002.

Coutinho, Ashley(2007), "Shop, Skip and Jump", *Brand Equity, Economic Times*, 20 September, 2006.

Dave, D. Weatherspoon and Thomas Reardon (2006) *A Study on the Rise in Supermarkets in Africa*, Michigan State University.

Dominique, Nanthini (2007), "The Brand Conscious Puducherrian", *The Hindu*, Saturday, March 24, 2007.

Edward, Cundiff (1995), "Concepts in Comparative Retailing" *Journal of Marketing*, 1995.

Feuer, J (2005), "Retailing Grows up, Looks to Image – Building", *Ad Week*, Vol. 16, No: 9, p. 8.

ICICI Bank Report (2004), "Foreign Direct Investment in Retail", Study Report Published by ICICI, 2004.

Majumdar, D. (2007), "FDI in Retailing: India as a Supermarket" *Business Standard*, 2007.

Mehta, Sandhya (2006), "Up Coming Malls – Shoppers Paradise", The ICFAI University Press, Marketing Mastermind, November 2006, pp. 49-5.

Morris, Tim (2001), "Retail Supermarket Globalization Who's Winning?", Careolis Research Group Analysis, 2001.

Padmapriya, J. (2007), "Shopping Mania", *Brand Equity*, Economic Times, February, 2007.

Papu, Ravi and Pascale RW (2007), "Does Customer Satisfaction Lead to Improved Brand Equity? – An Empirical Examination of Two Categories of Retail Brands", *The ICFAI Journal of Brand Management*, March 20007, Vol. IV, No. 1, pp. 44-62.

Pappu R. and Cooksey (2005), "Consumer Based Brand Equity Improving the Measurement – Empirical Evidence", *Journal of Product and Brand Management*, Vol. 14, No. 3 pp. 143-154.

Prayag, Anjali (2007), "Retail Lessons – Indians Prefer to Discover and Converse", *The Hindu*, p. 5, Business Line 2007.

Ramanathan, Anand and Manu Parashar (2006) "A Typology of Format Adaptation Strategies in Comparative Retailing" Research Paper from IIM, Bangalore, 2006.

The Hindu, "Nilgris to Expand Franchisee Network" Business Line, February 13, 2007.

The Hindu, "Retail, Media, FMCG will be Active Hiring Sectors in Q1" April 10, p. 5, Business Line.

Vikas and Bharathy tamilan (2007), "The Meeting of the Extremes", *Nanayam Magazine*, 1-15 April 2007.

Performance of Cadbury's Bournvita in Comparison to its Competitors in Twin Cities of Bhubaneswar and Cuttack
A Case Study

Samarendra Mahapatra*

INTRODUCTION

Fact File

Cadbury employes 60,000 people in over 200 countries.

Cadbury the worlds No. 1 Confectionery company.

Cadbury the worlds No. 2 Gums company.

Cadbury the worlds No 3 beverage company.

Bournvita Exclusive

Cadbury was incorporated in India on 19th July, 1948 as a private limited company under the name of Cadbury-Fry (India). Cadbury Bournvita was launched during the

* IMIS, Bhubaneswar, Orissa.

same year. It is among the oldest brands in the malt-based food/malt food category with a rich heritage and has always been known to provide the best nutrition to aid growth and all round development. Throughout it's history, Cadbury Bournvita has continuously re-invented itself in terms of product, packaging, promotion and distribution.

The Success Mantra

The brand has been an enduring symbol of mental and physical health ever since it was launched in 1948. It is hardly surprising then, that Bournvita enjoys a major presence in the Malt Food market. Given its market share of 17 per cent, Cadbury Bournvita reaches across hundreds of cities, towns and villages through 3,50,000 outlets in India. It is a universal truth that mothers attach a lot of emotional importance to nourishment while bringing up their children.

It is a case to find out the market performance of Cadbury's Bournvita in the markets of Bhubaneswar and Cuttack by undertaking a comparative study taking three other competitors from the health drink sector *viz.* Horlicks, Complan and Boost. It has enabled to understand the market performance of the product in comparison to these competitors through market share and market penetration data. The methodology applied in the process was through a retail audit undertaken in 300 and 200 samples in Bhubaneswar and Cuttack respectively. A customer survey was carried out on 50 customers to understand the customer's perception about the product and the reasons for them choosing a brand of health drink over others.

OBJECTIVE, SCOPE AND LIMITATION

Objective of the Study

The central objectives of the study are:

- To find out the market performance of Cadbury's Bournvita through market share and market penetration statistics.

- To make a comparative analysis of performance of four brand of health drinks along with Bournvita.
- To determine the reasons for the downward trend of the product in the market and find some suitable remedial measures.
- To undertake a customer audit to have a fair idea about the perception of customers towards Cadbury's Bournvita as a health drink.

Scope of the Study

The study that was undertaken during later part of 2007 was limited to the markets of Cuttack and Bhubaneswar. Thus, this study is not an extensive study of the overall market performance of Bournvita in the whole of the country. Moreover, through this study it was determined the market share and market penetration of Bournvita to analyse its performance in comparison to its competitors. Lastly the study was conducted on only 200 and 300 samples of Cuttack and Bhubaneswar respectively which is a very nominal proportion of the total population.

Limitations of the Study

The major limitations of the study are:

- There are some other health-drinks brands in the market but only the major competitors of Bournvita are taken into consideration.
- Due to time constraints only 300 and 200 samples from Bhubaneswar and Cuttack are taken respectively.
- Study was only on the major markets of Bhubaneswar and Cuttack and not all markets.
- The number of non respondents was about 15 per cent and 18 per cent of the samples in Cuttack and Bhubaneswar respectively.

The Levels of Competition

There are primarily four levels of competition, namely; product form competition, product category competition, generic competition and budget competition. In this project author has concentrated his efforts only on product form competition and ignored the other forms of competition, Bournvita as a product faces:

(a) Product form competition

(b) Product category competition

(c) Generic competition

(d) Budget competition.

RESEARCH METHODOLOGY

The central aim of the study was:

- To find out the market performance of Bournvita in comparison to its competitors in the markets of Cuttack and Bhubaneswar.
- To find out the perception of customers towards Bournvita as a health drink.

DATA COLLECTION

Author has collected both primary and secondary data in order to fulfil his objectives. In order to complete the first aim author has collected primary data from the various retailers of both Cuttack and Bhubaneswar. Author has also collected data from distributors of Cadbury in Cuttack. Author has collected secondary data from organizational websites and other related sites.

In order to complete the second aim author has collected primary data from 50 customers of different age groups through a questionnaire developed by author.

The study conducted during the summer project was basically a Marketing Research which is the systematic and objective identification, collection, analysis, dissemination, and use of information for the purpose of improving decision-making related to the identification and solution of problems and opportunities in marketing of Bournvita as a health drink.

SAMPLING DESIGN

Target Population

The target population who was identified for collection of primary data were the retailers of various outlets who deal with the concerned products, for the purpose of fulfilling the first aim. In case of the second aim, data was collected from various customers of different age group.

The retail outlets were divided into three categories namely; A, B, C depending on the floor space available in the outlets. Author had also restricted my survey to four types of outlets *viz.* medicine shops, general stores, kirana shops and departmental stores. The purpose of this division was to achieve a more in depth and extensive analysis of the findings.

Sampling Frame

Author has collected data by visiting various shops in the markets of Cuttack and Bhubaneswar who deal with either Bournvita or any of its competing health drinks. For the customer survey author has surveyed people from different age groups in Big Bazaar.

SAMPLING TECHNIQUE

1. For retail audit: simple random sampling.
2. For customer audit: stratified sampling.

SAMPLE SIZE

Cuttack		
Total no. of shops visited	:	233
Number of non respondents	:	37

Bhubaneswar		
Total no. of shops visited	:	302
Number of non respondents	:	42

Research Type

The type of research undertaken was essentially a descriptive research.

Research Design

Qualitative research methodology is unstructured, exploratory in nature, based on small samples, and may utilize popular qualitative techniques, which provide insights and understanding of the problem setting.

Qualitative Research Method

Questionnaire and retail audit sheet.

THE BHUBANESWAR MARKET: MARKET SHARE

Total Market Share of Bournvita in Bhubaneswar

The total number of outlets visited in Bhubaneswar was 300. The data analysis is done on the basis of these 300 outlets. The major competitors who are taken into account for the comparative analysis are Horlicks, Complan and Boost. The data analysis done here is by taking all the SKUs together for both Bournvita as well as its competitors.

Market share of Bournvita	:	24.14
Market share of Horlicks	:	59.79
Market share of Complan	:	13.99
Market share of Boost	:	2.06

Findings

1. The overall market share of Bournvita is 24 per cent.
2. Horlicks leads the market with 60 per cent market share.
3. Complan lags behind at 14 per cent market share.

Market Share of Bournvita on the basis of SKUs

Only Bournvita and Complan has 200 g SKUs in the market. The 500 g SKU is available for all the brands taken in to consideration. Only Bournvita and Horlicks have 1 kg SKUs in the market.

Market share of 200 gm SKU

Market share of 200 g Bournvita	:	73.89
Market share of 200 g Complan	:	26.10

Findings

Market share of 200 g Bournvita in the Bhubaneswar markets is a healthy 74 per cent, as compared to Complan's 26 per cent.

Market share of 500 gm SKU

Market share of 500 g Bournvita	:	25.53
Market share of 500 g Horlicks	:	48.56
Market share of 500 g Complan	:	21.95
Market share of 500 g Boost	:	3.94

Findings

1. Market share of Bournvita in this SKU is 26 per cent. While Complan is a close competitor.
2. Horlicks is the leader in this SKU with 48 per cent market share.
3. Boost stands nowhere with a mere market share of 4 per cent.

Market share of 1 kg SKU

Market share of 1 kg Bournvita	:	14.51
Market share of 1 kg Horlicks	:	85.48

Findings

Bournvita doesn't have a much prominent market share in the 1 kg SKU with a nominal market share of 15 per cent only.

Market Share on the Basis of Category

The outlets that were visited have been divided in to categories namely; A, B, C on the basis of the floor space that is available in the outlets.

(a) maximum space;

(b) medium space;

(c) minimum space

This is an analysis of the market share of Bournvita in comparison to its competitors in the various category of outlets combining all its SKUs.

Market Share of Bournvita and its Competitors for All SKUs in A Category Counters

Market share of Bournvita for all SKU	:	25.76
Market share of Horlicks for all SKU	:	56.19
Market share of Complan for all SKU	:	14.26
Market share of Boost for all SKU	:	3.77

Findings

1. Bournvita is significantly ahead of Complan in the A category outlets.
2. Horlicks has a clear lead in terms of market share with 56 per cent market share.
3. Complan has 14 per cent market share in A category shops.

Market Share of Bournvita and its Competitors for All SKU's in B Category Counters

Market share of Bournvita for all SKU	:	22.73
Market share of Horlicks for all SKU	:	60.62
Market share of Complan for all SKU	:	14.75
Market share of Boost for all SKU	:	1.88

Findings

1. Bournvita has a market share of 23 per cent.
2. Horlicks has a market share of 60 per cent in B category stores.
3. Complan has 15 per cent market share in B category shops.

Market Share of Bournvita and its Competitors for All SKUs in C Category Counters

Market share of Bournvita for all SKU	:	24.58
Market share of Horlicks for all SKU	:	64.94
Market share of Complan for all SKU	:	10.00
Market share of Boost for all SKU	:	0.46

Findings

1. Bournvita is in the second place in terms of market share.
2. Horlicks is the out and out leader with a market share of 65 per cent.
3. Complan merely finds foot in this category of outlets.

THE CUTTACK MARKET: MARKET SHARE

Total Market Share of Bournvita in Cuttack

The total number of outlets visited in Cuttack is 196. The data analysis done is on the basis of these 196 samples.

The major competitors who are taken into account for the comparative analysis are Horlicks, Complan and Boost. The data analysis done here is by taking all the SKU's together for both Bournvita as well as its competitors.

Market share of Bournvita	:	16.25
Market share of Horlicks	:	68.45
Market share of Complan	:	14.12
Market share of Boost	:	1.16

Findings

1. Horlicks has the maximum market share in Cuttack in terms of sales with a huge lead over Bournvita.
2. Bournvita and Complan are approximately in the balance wheel in terms of market share.
3. However Boost is reeling at the bottom of the chart with per cent market share.

Market Share on the Basis of SKUs in Cuttack

Only Bournvita and Complan has 200 g SKUs in the market. The 500 g SKUs is available for all the brands taken in to consideration. Only Bournvita and Horlicks have 1 kg SKUs in the market.

Market Share of 200 g SKU

Market share of 200 g Bournvita	:	57.15
Market share of 200 g Complan	:	42. 84

Findings

Bournvita is the out and out market leader in this SKU as revealed from the chart.

Market Share of 500 g SKU

Market share of 500 gm Bournvita	:	16.92
Market share of 500 gm Horlicks	:	63.05

Market share of 500 gm Complan	:	18.29
Market share of 500 gm Boost	:	1.72

Findings

1. Bournvita has marginally shifted from its second position in the 500 g SKU and conceded its position to Complan as revealed from the study.
2. Horlicks lead the market with 63 per cent market share in the 500 g SKU.
3. Boost doesn't appear to be a threat with two per cent market share.

Market Share of 1 kg SKU

Market share of 1 kg Bournvita	:	6.83
Market share of 1 kg Horlicks	:	93.16

Findings

Bournvita struggles to compete with Horlicks in this SKU where there is a huge difference in the market share between the two, as found out by the research.

Market Share on the Basis of Category

The outlets that were visited have been divided into categories namely; A, B, C on the basis of the floor space that is available in the outlets.

(a) maximum space

(b) medium space;

(c) minimum space

This is an analysis of the market share of Bournvita in comparison to its competitors in the various category of outlets combining all its SKUs.

Market Share of Bournvita and its Competitors for All SKUs in A Category Counters

Market share of Bournvita in all SKU	:	18.89
Market share of Horlicks in all SKU	:	65.01
Market share of Complan in all SKU	:	14.31
Market share of Boost in all SKU	:	1.78

Findings

1. Bournvita has a fair market share of 19 per cent in the A category shops.
2. Horlicks leads the market with a huge market share of 65 per cent.

Market Share of Bournvita and its Competitors for All SKUs in B Category Counters

Market share of Bournvita in all SKU	:	14.73
Market share of Horlicks in all SKU	:	70.33
Market share of Complan in all SKU	:	14.15
Market share of Boost in all SKU	:	0.78

Findings

1. Market share of Bournvita and Complan are hovering around the same percentage as revealed from the graph.
2. Horlicks has the maximum market share in B type counters with a market share of 70 per cent.
3. Boost is again reeling at one per cent market share.

Market Share of Bournvita and its Competitors for All SKUs in C Category Counters

Market share of Bournvita for all SKU	:	11.40
Market share of Horlicks for all SKU	:	75.29
Market share of Complan for all SKU	:	11.96
Market share of Boost for all SKU	:	1.33

Findings

1. Again Bournvita and Complan go neck to neck in terms of market share with 11 per cent and 12 per cent market share respectively.
2. Horlicks has a hoping lead of 76 per cent as found out from the market survey in the C category outlets.

Market Share on the Basis of the Types of Outlets Visited

During the course of the research the outlets that were visited have been divided into four types namely General, Kirana, Medicine and Departmental stores.

Total market share of Bournvita in each type of shop was determined. Along with it market share is also found out for each SKU segment in the specified types of outlets visited.

Market Share of Bournvita for All SKU in the General Stores

Market share of Bournvita for all SKU	:	25.48
Market share of Horlicks for all SKU	:	59.27
Market share of Complan for all SKU	:	13.62
Market share of Boost for all SKU	:	1.60

Findings

1. Market share of Bournvita is a healthy 25 per cent in the general stores.
2. Though Horlicks remains the market leader with 59 per cent share.

Market Share of Bournvita for All SKU in the Kirana Stores

Market share of Bournvita for all SKU	:	18.40
Market share of Horlicks for all SKU	:	65.55

Market share of Complan for all SKU	:	15.21
Market share of Boost for all SKU	:	0.82

Findings

1. Bournvita has a market share of above 18 per cent a lead over Complan having a market share of 15.21 per cent.
2. Horlicks enjoys a market share of 66 per cent in the kirana stores.
3. Boost has failed to raise its market share in the kirana type outlets as well.

Market Share of Bournvita for All SKU in the Medical Stores

Market share of Bournvita in all SKU	:	3.04
Market share of Horlicks in all SKU	:	82.27
Market share of Complan in all SKU	:	13.70
Market share of Boost in all SKU	:	0.98

Findings

1. Bournvita hardly finds existence in the medical stores in terms of market share data as provided above.
2. Horlicks is the leader in the market with Complan.
3. Boost with 1% market share is just behind Bournvita!

Market Share of Bournvita of All SKU in Departmental Stores

Market share of Bournvita in all SKU	:	33.81
Market share of Horlicks in all SKU	:	50.29
Market share of Complan in all SKU	:	13.89
Market share of Boost in all SKU	:	1.99

Findings

1. Market share of Bournvita is a healthy 34 per cent.
2. Horlicks has a distinct lead of 50 per cent in the market.
3. Complan has a market share of 14 per cent.

CONCLUSION

The analysis thus done shows clearly that Bournvita has not performed as expected in the markets of Bhubaneswar and Cuttack. It is due to certain factors which have come up during the course of the research which needs to be addressed. The findings of the market research are later illustrated along with certain recommendations to make sure Bournvita reaches the zenith in the health drink sector once again.

FINDINGS

1. Bournvita as a health drink is not the first name that comes to a customer's mind. This is confirmed through the customer audit that was done on 50 customers. The percentage of customers who remembered of the brand as a top of the mind brand recall is 30 per cent compared to people remembering Horlicks which is 40 per cent.
2. Overall market share of Bournvita in Cuttack is 16.25 per cent compared to Horlicks which is 68.45 per cent. The overall market share of Bournvita in Bhubaneswar is compared to Horlicks which is 60 per cent.
3. Overall market penetration of Bournvita in Cuttack is 61 per cent compared to Horlicks which is 97 per cent. The overall market penetration of Bournvita in the Bhubaneswar is 85 per cent compared to Horlicks which is 97 per cent.
4. Market share of Bournvita is less in certain C category shops because the distributors tend to ignore the C category shop as they don't have high volume sales.

5. Market share and penetration of Bournvita is less in certain small markets such as Tankapani Road and Old Station Road in Bhubaneswar and Nimachouri and Bjrakabati in Cuttack because the distributors are irregular in these markets.

6. One complain from the retailers side in some cases have been that distributors don't replace damaged and expired products. One such incident has been illustrated below.

7. Display is not got by 90 per cent of the retailers, thus the customers don't get to see the product at the first instence when they visit the shops.

8. There are not enough ads and promotions undertaken. As a result both distributors and customers don't get to know about new products much.

9. Bournvita as a product is tremendously under positioned in the customers mind. It is perceived by most people that it is a children's drink rather than a health drink. Moreover, it is not frequently prescribed by doctors as a health drink. It is for this reason that interestingly a number of medical stores do not keep the product even though Horlicks is kept.

10. To understand the cause of less demand a customer audit was done which shows that about 56 per cent respondents said that they don't get influenced by the advertisements of Bournvita. This problem needs to be addressed.

SUGGESTIONS

1. Cadburys might consider the positioning of Bournvita as a health drink rather than a children's drink. This can be achieved though various promotional activities which would portray the product as a health drink.

2. It is possible to position Bournvita through the doctors and physicians if its possible to convince them that

Bournvita contains all the food values that a health drink should possess.

3. Promotional activities can be taken more efficiently so that new product information can be reached to retailers and customers more efficiently.

4. Display can be provided to every retailer or at least posters can be provided to the retailers so that customer's buying decision can be influenced.

5. The company can consider speaking to the distributors to address the problems relating to them.

6. Bournvita seems to have ignored its market potential in C category shops. It can reconsider its efforts towards these small shops to reach the position of Horlicks.

7. It is seen that the market penetration of Bournvita is much less in *kirana* type stores as compared to its presence in other type of stores. Thus efforts can be directed to improve its penetration in smaller shops through promotional activities.

8. Retailers can be given higher incentives like regular distribution and higher profit margin etc. to promote Bournvita as a brand so that some degree of push selling is also takes place through them.

REFERENCES

Aaker, *Marketing Research*.

Kothari, C.R, *Research Methodology*.

Gupta, S.P., *Statistics*.

9

Information Technology in Retail Management

A Tool for Growth of Retail Sector

Rajib Lochan Panigrahy*

ABSTRACT

Retailing is a most established branch of marketing. Retail marketing begins with understanding of shopping behaviour and its impact on formulating and implementing loyalty programme. So, there are two specific dimensions to retail marketing, first is to create retail environment, i.e. shop, market, restaurant, mall, etc. and second is how to attract customers to purchase from that outlet. Today's retail market become sophisticated in the tune of competition, customer demand and for the means of loyalty. Most of the retail shops, outlets, malls and multi-dimensional with IT technology are virtual internet stores. This attracts customers, motivate, buying behaviour stimulate customers to buy.

* Faculty (MBA), Ambedkar College of Management & Technology, Berhampur, Orissa.

General merchandise retailers, food retailers (grocery) and e-retails are the three broad retail categories that one finds in the retail sector. In India Food retailer (grocery) is popularly known as retail market and is dominated the retail market sector. Excessive competition in the food retailing sector would drive prospective retailing sector investors to choose special retailing. Greater prospects possible to speciality stores and chances of rapid development for new products enable specialities. It is a wheel of retailing theory to emerge in the field. So, there is a chance of rise in speciality retailing in India. The penetration of internet in India is minimal and therefore e-retailing (IT in Retailing) is confined to a small minority in urban areas.

INTRODUCTION

Retailing had started since civilisation incepted. Firstly it was barter system as a medium of exchange of goods against goods. As the civilisation has developed interaction between producer and customer gave birth to customer interaction. Hence, any business to customer interaction is termed as retailing. Retailing was dealt with retailer as one of the channel members of the distribution. The supply chain management has to make the distinction between traditional retailing and professional retailing. The traditional retailing is the case of local provision stores known as retail shops or kirana shops. And the supply chain still rests with the marketers, decision of retailing can not be independent. In this situation and the relationship among marketers, suppliers, vendors, rests on traditional retailers. In professional/organised retailing the control of supply chain is performer by retailers. The control of supply chain by the retailer could be due to the uniqueness of the products or services, the retailer provides or due to the enormous clout enjoyed by the retailer on account of its presence across a region or a country through a chain of stores. The number of stores implies the number of consumers. With whom the retailer interacts with and has information about as well as the huge volume of purchase i.e. possible with a large chain. The business of the retail management could be analyses to the media i.e space selling of the newspaper or print media or time selling of electronic media called as advertising. Real estate management also a proxy retail business successful running of a retail business is not possible without understanding all. The major sub-disciplines of management viz. operations management, human resource management, marketing management. Operations management forms one of the key function of retailing as the supply chain which interacts and transacts between supplier/vendor and the chain store corporate headquarters or the individual stores, inventory management and logistics, specific activities that take place from the production of goods and/or services to the consumption and feedbacks from the customers are to be managed by the retailers.

CHALLENGES AND OPPORTUNITIES OF RETAILING

Retailing provides considerable value to the consumers. It provides opportunities to people to grow and change their career for rewarding and challenging in jobs. Evidences world wide envisaged that the economies enjoyed social and economic progress has strong retail sectors because retailing has emerged a good portion of GDP. It is estimated that retail sector accounts for 10 per cent of GDP in western countries. Amongst developing countries, retailing in India accounts 10 of its GDP and China accounts 8 per cent GDP. On the whole the future of retailing in developing countries including India is promising. In India increasing middle class people, increase in income, urbanisation and migration of people from rural to urban – increasing urban population, improved communication facility to rural areas, i.e. road, telephony, television media, etc., technological revolution and globalisation are fuelling growth of retailing sector. However, the growth of big corporate retailers, foreign and domestic, are posing serious challenges of survival of 98 per cent of small and unorganised/traditional retailers in India, the following table envisages the facts.

Table 9.1: Global Retail Industry

Sl. No.	Country	Size in Billion US $	Share of Organised Retail Industry	Share of Organised Retail Industry
1.	U.S.A.	2325	85%	15%
2.	Taiwan	115	81%	19%
3.	Malaysia	20	55%	45%
4.	Thailand	22	40%	60%
5.	Brazil	100	36%	46%
6.	Indonesia	75	30%	70%
7.	Poland	55	20%	80%
8.	China	325	20%	80%
9.	India	180	2%	98%
10.	South Korea		15%	85%
11.	Philippines		35%	65%

Moreover the issues like needs for adequate investment, trained manpower, appropriate modern technology, retail mix model, regional inequalities, 24 hour retailing, etc. are to be added in right perspective for on-going economic reforms and consequent liberalisation in the country.

In India, the retail sector is the second largest employer after agricultural sector. The retailing sector in India is highly fragmented and consists predominantly of small, independent and self-managed shops. The trend of retail business in last years has shown the encouraging scene of the retail sector in future which will emerge the growth of the economy, employment generating in both organised and unorganised sector. The Table 9.2 envisages the growth of retail business in last decade.

Table 9.2: Growth of Retail Business in India (1990-00 to 2009-10)

Year	Retailing Business in India (INR in Crores)
1999-2000	5000
2003-2004	15000
2005-2006	35000
2009-2010	60800

Source: The Orissa Journal of Commerce, Vol. XXX, No. 2, 2008, p. 83.

A strong trend in favour of organised retail format is being witnessed in both food and non-food retail sectors as customers showing preference for ambience and convenience in shopping in one shop. In future time will be constraint for shopping and trend of shopping will grownup. Hence, one-stop-shop will be mostly preferred for the customers. So, the growth of retail sector emerged super markets and centrally air-conditioned shopping malls are opening gradually. Before 1990s, shopping malls in India are Ansal Plaza in New Delhi, Cross Road in Mumbai, Spencer's Plaza in Chennai. In post- 1990s there are many retail giants opening their malls, hubs, outlets in India. There are 1500 super markets, 11.025 departmental stores, 300 shopping malls by 2004. It is expected that 800 more malls will be opened by 2010 round the country and it may be more than this as the increasing trend of opening and customer preference is found. The shopping malls in India has been increased to 350 by 2009 from 25 in 2003.

India is a fastest growing country retail sector indicated the Global Retail Development Index (GRDI) released by A.T Kearney showing attractiveness of investment in retail sector among 30 emerging markets across the globe . It indicates that India is the most attractive market for investment flowing into retail industry. Hence, retailing has already been looked at a prospective area for Foreign Direct Investment (FDI). Government has also promoting investment in supply chains and infrastructure like real estate through FDI to facilitate retail growth. It is evidentiary that after a decade of China permitting FDI in retail sector, the sector has increased 20 per cent from 10 per cent in organised retiling. It is a method of transfer of finance, technology, knowledge and skill into domestic retail sector. It is find that due to FDI, India has grown GDP by 8 per cent in 10th Plan i.e. 2002-2007. India is an emerging FDI destination which has taken 2nd position after China. The Table 9.3 depicts the 10 FDI destinations.

Table 9.3: Key FDI Destinations

Sl. No.	Country	Rank in 2004	Rank in 2005
1.	China	1	1
2.	India	3	2
3.	U.S.A.	2	3
4.	U.K.	4	4
5.	Poland	12	5
6.	Russia	11	6
7.	Brazil	17	7
8.	Australia	7	8
9.	Germany	5	9
10.	Hong Kong	8	10

Source: AT Kearney, *The Times of India*, December 9, 2005.

It has more opportunities of economic growth and employment in organised and unorganised sector both in rural and urban areas. In India retail industry is a largest private industry where 5 lakh of people are engaged in organised retail industry and 4 crores of people are engaged in unorganised retail sector. Day-by-day the organised retailing industries will grow-up and the employment level will be grown up. Hence, it is potential as an employment generating sector both in organised professionals and unorganised workers. Indian retail sector has contributes 10 per cent of its GDP and 6 per cent of total employment of the country which shows in Table 9.4.

Table 9.4: Retail Industry's Contribution to GDP and Employment

Sl. No.	Country	Share in GDP (%)	Share in Employment (%)
1.	USA	9.4	16.7
2.	Poland	11.0	14.7
3.	China	8.0	12.0
4.	Brazil	6.4	6.0
5.	India	10.0	6.0

Source: CII-Mckinsy Report.

RETAIL BANKING

India is one of the fastest growing economies in the world after over a decade of financial and banking sector reforms since 1991. Evidence from across the world suggests that a sound and evolved banking system is required for sustained economic development. So, there is a great need of retail banking which refers that the commercial banks dealing with individual customer, both on liabilities and assets sides of the balance sheet, fixed/current/savings bank accounts on the liabilities side and mortgage loans like personal, housing, construction, automobiles and educational on the asset side with ancillary services including credit cards, debit cards, depository services including personal loans belongs to agriculture, trade, industry and shop on consumer durable goods. The major players of retail banking among the commercial banks are Centurion Bank of Punjab, ICICI Bank, Bank of India, Dena Bank, Allahabad Bank, Fullerton, HDFC Bank, HSBC Bank, Religare, DBS Cholamandalam, etc. Most of the factors responsible for growth of retail banking is possible due to introduction of technology and opening of private banks with perfect competition among bank services. With technological advancements, retail banking marched ahead towards economic development of Indian economy. Multi-national banks able to deliver quality services and a sophisticated portfolio of financial products might create an opening in this wall of loyalty and capture a share of India's fast-growing retail banking sector.

APPAREAL RETAILING

India is the 4th largest economy in terms of purchasing power parity (PPP) after U.S.A., China and Japan and is rated among the top 10 FDI destinations. The Indian textile and appareal is also experiencing rapid change and growth. Appareal has the largest share of the modern organised retail sector in India, i.e. 36 per cent of the current market (June 2006). The appareal sector is generally labour intensive with non-formal/unorganised/less skilled labourers with low wage payment strata. In the high quality fashion market, this industry is characterised by modern technology, relatively well-paid workers and designers and a high degree of flexibility. It is one of the largest foreign exchange earners for nearly 20 per cent of country's total export which was $9.5 billion in last 2006-2007 FY. So, it is key revenue driven for organised retailing in India with mostly unorganised workers. The segment is witnessing growth on account of increasing income level, increase in proportion of working women against others.

Clothing and textile dominated the market accounted 36 per cent of total organised retailing followed by watches and jewellery, i.e. 17 per cent. This is indicative of the opportunity for organised retail growth in these segments (Table 9.5). The proliferation of hyper market and super markets has led to a growth in food and grocery retail, thus value retailing is seen to be gaining ground in India. Appareal retailing has gained momentum in retail sector by producing school uniform, general dresses, traditional dresses to made up garments of high quality by local tailors marketed by high class shopping firms. The appareal retails has increased to 2715 in 2007 from 1350 in 2002 and appareal chain stores to 3919 in 2007 from 2469 in 2002 and single large stores ready made garments in rural India has been increasing rapidly. It is obviously demanded in urban areas.

Table 9.5: Contribution of Different Categories to Organised Retail in 2007

Sectors of Retail	Shares of Contribution (%)
Food and Grocery	14
Footwear	13
Durables	10
Jewellery and Watches	17
Appareal (clothing & textiles)	36
Book, Music & Gifts	3
Others	7

Source: Economists.com, Sygnus Research.

IT IN RETAILING

The term "retail is in the detail" aptly sums up the significance of each path of operations involved from the vendor to the customer as well as the feedback loop back to the vendor as retailing is a consumer interfacing activities and acts as a last link in the supply chain, it is where data generated about the customers and about products and services could be of immense help for members across the supply chain. As product and service categories, the date could be collected increases by the leaps and bounds. Traditional retailers depend on personal memory to record customer and product information, but as retailing become a professional and widespread enterprise, personal memory started to fail and therefore a need for technology to record data for analysis emerged. Information Technology (IT), therefore, is a one of the great enablers of efficient and effective retailing. It keeps greater transparency and professionalism in dealing with supply chain issues, dealing with operations management. Technology for data warehousing and development of data mining and development of expert systems were the initial developments that later developed into a full-fledged retail ERP (Entrepreneur Resource Planning) that integrated all the components of the retail business and helped to provide a steamless view of the impact of changed of parameters to the retail business. Thus, in view of the data intensive and operations oriented nature of the businesses, retailing involves a strong complement of IT management both of the hardware as well as the software.

The IT is one of the greatest enablers of the collaboration between the vendor and retailers. It passes the influence to get manufacturers, into collaborative e-business, because it can represent more attractive media of business. It is an environment, where greater data transparency and information sharing as well as the speed keeps between supplier retailer relationship. It is find that it is more helpful to fashion conscious sector of retailing, this represents challenges in a style oriented business. It implies heavy dependence on technology and highly skilled workforce support that would make information sharing a smooth affairs. Retailer sales announcement have an effect on the security price of suppliers. It has a greater transparency in information sharing as mandatory by law. It include purchase record, complementary of future expectations, cooperation and adoption between both the parties.

CONCLUSION

India is a place of rapid change in its economic growth and prosperity towards developed county. Retail sector is a tool of growth of GDP and employment which attracts the FDI giants and foreign retailer enter into the economy which can flow the finance, technology, skill, knowledge and can compete the domestic retailers towards sustainability with their own resources and developing themselves. Retail business became a buzzword. Most of the sectors related to marketing has been entering into the retail sector as an associate/business partner for their business promotion. There is a need of maintaining customer care service not only in name to attract the customers but in reality as they promise. Retailing posed emerging trend in appareal, fashion, restaurant, jewellery, furniture, hotel and tourism, home décor, grocery, cellular phones and services, durable consumer goods, real estate, insurance products, bank schemes/services, etc. with the services of Postal, Courier, Banks, Insurance Companies (Group/Life/Non-Life), Telephone/Cellular Service Providers, Hotels, etc. The retail market has emerged with the help of Information Technology (IT) which has made the communication easier with telephonic services via on-line enquiry, SMS, internet, tele-services for home/door delivery, online payments, online fund transfers from ATM or Debit Card/Credit Card enabled machines in retail trade centres, tele-banking, internet banking, etc. with web-enabled services like email, downloading, browsing, chatting not only through internet but also through pocket internet that is internet in cellular phones/mobiles. In the technological advancements, retail sector will grow towards an emerging sector in Indian economy.

REFERENCES

Jena, Arta Bandhu, Misra Devi Prasad, Retail Marketing in India: The Emerging Issues and Challenges, *The Orissa Journal of Commerce*, Vol. XXX, No. 2, 2008, pp. 137-146.

Lall, G.S., Misra P.C., The Organised Retail Boom and Foreign Direct Investment, *The Orissa Journal of Commerce*, Vol. XXX; No. 2, 2008, p. 169-173.

Mohanty, A.K., Panda J, Retailing in India: Challenges and Opportunities, *The Orissa Journal of Commerce*, Vol. XXIX, No. 2, 2008, pp. 69-80.

Panda, A.K., Mohanty S, Emerging Retail Trends in India, *The Orissa Journal of Commerce*, Vol. XXX, No. 2, 2008, pp. 81-89.

Sivakumar, A., *Retail Marketing* (2007), Excel Books, New Delhi.

Sygnus Business Consulting and Research 2008, p. 276.

10

Supply and Demand Forecast of the Bhutan Tourism

Achintya Mahapatra*
Umesh Namdev Jadhav*

The Tourism Council of Bhutan (TCB), in keeping with the tourism policy "High value-low volume', categories accommodations as per the "Regulation for Accommodation of Tourists, 1999'. Under these Regulations there are three different categories: A, B and C. However, to cater to regional tourists the TCB has developed, informally, a fourth category that targets regional tourists and are classified under regional category hotels. However, soon this system of categorization will be replaced by the international "star" classification system. With this new classification system more number of hotels will be encouraged to upgrade their facilities and services.

Bhutan is in a very fortunate position in terms of tourism. The tourism industry has created a wide range of

* Sr. Lecturer, Department of Business Studies, Royal University of Bhutan.

opportunities for Bhutanese who have begun to grasp economic opportunities offered by the industry. Tourism has also been a self-financing mechanism for promoting the country's environment and facilitating an awareness and understanding of the uniqueness of this country. Tourism has resulted in some adverse impacts but the government has recognized the need to address them. Tourism has also promoted Bhutanese culture by creating employment opportunities for traditional musicians and dancers and encouraged the revival of local festivals in different parts of the country. The private sector is being more involved in not only monitoring itself but also in developing future tourism policies. Tourism bodies like the Tourism Development Committee and the Association of Bhutanese Tour Operators have been established to foster partnership between relevant sectors involved in the industry and within the industry itself. So far the government's policy of "high value-low volume" tourism has been successful in regulating the growth of the industry and maintaining the number of visitors at an acceptable level.

Only the government can provide the strategic planning base for tourism and ensure that valuable and fragile habitats are identified, that baseline monitoring is carried out, and that the overall needs and implications of tourism are assessed. Tourism will be sustainable only if tourism planners and operators give due consideration to the carrying capacity of our natural resources, recognize that people and communities, customs and lifestyles contribute to the tourism experience and, therefore, accept that these people should also get some of the benefits from tourism.

Additional Accommodation Providers

Table 10.2 shows that almost all hotels proposed or under construction are in western and central Bhutan where there is already huge number of hotels. This is a serious problem if tourist arrivals do not increase or unless these upcoming hotels intend to target regional and domestic tourists. If this trend continues, it is very likely that hoteliers will slowly compromise their service and facilities to cut down on room rates. If this happens. It will serve as a threat to the government's "high value low volume" policy.

Table 10.1: Categories of Accommodation Providers

Dzongkhag	Grade A Hotels	Grade B Hotels	Grade C Hotels	Regional
Paro	2	17	8	3
Thimphu	7	13	2	13
Bumthang	1	7	7	2
Punakha	0	4	1	2
Wang/Phodrang	1	4	2	0
Trongsa	1	2	0	0
Chhukha	1	3	1	4
Trashigang	0	0	2	0
Monggar	0	2	1	2
Haa	0	1	1	1
S/Jongkhar	0	1	2	1
Tsirang	0	0	1	1
Total	**13**	**54**	**28**	**29**

In 2008, there were 46 hotels proposed and under construction compared to 42 hotels in 2007. Out of 42 hotels proposed or under construction in 2007, total of 11 were completed in 2008, including regional hotels. With another 46 hotels there will be an additional of 1704 beds available for tourists' consumption.

TELECOMMUNICATION INFRASTRUCTURE

Internet facilities available in the town of Bhutan, B-Mobile and Tashi cell coverage of all the districts except remote place like Merak and Sengteng, Laya and Lingzhi and high some of the villages in Bhutan however B-mobile has covered almost all the parts of the country except Tashi cell. And by the year 2014 the Tashi and B-mobile have plan to connect all the parts of the country.

Table 10.2: Additional Accommodation Providers.

Dzongkhag	New hotels (Under Construction and Proposed)	Additional Rooms	Additional Beds
Thimphu	10	250	484
Paro	17	320	610
Punakha	3	62	91
Trongsa	2	46	92
Bumthang	9	145	290
Wangdi Phodrang	3	47	93
Laya	1	10	20
Phuntsholing	1	12	24
Total	**46**	**892**	**1704**

Source: Annual Report (Bhutan Tourism Monitor).

MODE OF TRANSPORTATION

Road and Air Accessibility

Accessibility continues to be a bottlenect for the tourism industry. Whilst some 88 per cent of all the visitors they come Druk air. The remaining they come from phuntsholing get way and Samdrup Jongkhar and Gelephu where these places are the only three main entry for the international people through overland by road.

The Government Bhutan has one international airport in Paro and by end of Tenth five-year plan the government has plan to operate domestic air in three different parts namely Yonphula (Trashigang), Bumthang and Gelephu (Sarpang). The international airport operates to 6 destinations namely Bangkok, Delhi, Kolkota, Dhaka, Kathmdhndu and Bodhgaya. At present Bhutan has three aircraft operating in international levels. The international tourists come from these routes. Bhutan has wide coverage of road connectivity of all the districts except Gasa. By the year 2020 Bhutan has policy to make two side high ways like Paro-Thimphu, Phuntsholing – Thimphu and Tashigang – Samdrup Jongkhar. Bhutan at present has 49 coaster bus plying different parts of the country.

VARIOUS TYPES OF TOURISM PRODUCTS IN BHUTAN

Medical Units

The government has maintained a system of complete free healthcare for not only the Bhutanese citizens but for also all those who reside in the country. In 1961 there was hardly any modern facility in Bhutan. Today the country has more than 29 hospitals, 160 Basic Health Units and 90 per cent health coverage with basic services. The health status of the population has remarkably improved, especially during the past ten years. The national healthcare delivery system is characterized by the central level being responsible for administration, training and major referrals, and the districts managing the delivery of basic services to the population through a network of district hospitals, Basic Health Units (BHU) and outreach clinics (ORC).

Modern Health Care

Modern healthcare was introduced in Bhutan in 1961. Until then, the people relied on a rich indigenous medicinal system known was *So-Wa-Rigpa* (wisdom of health) for preventive and curative measures. Buddhist rituals and the village *shaman* played an important role in health. In the Past three decades, the country saw great strides in the health sector. In 1961, there were only two hospitals (Thimphu and Samtse) and 11 dispensaries (Haa, Paro, Trongsa, Bumthang, Trashigang, Sipsoo, Tsirang, Samdrup Jongkhar, Kalikhola and Dagapela) and only two trained doctors in the whole country. Communicable diseases were wide-spread, and more than one-half of the children died at birth or within the first few years of their lives. Smallpox epidemic sometimes wiped out whole villages. In some parts of the country malaria claimed hundreds of lives each year, while in others diseases such as leprosy deformed and ultimately killed many people. Water supplies were largely confined to springs and streams.

Physical infrastructure today consists of four-tiered network of National Referral Hospital, Regional Referral Hospital, District Hospital and Basic Health Units. Currently, the country has more than 29 hospitals, 178 Basic Health Units and 519 Outreach Clinics (ORCs). The national healthcare delivery system is characterized by the central level being responsible for administration, training and major referrals and the Dzongkhag managing the delivery of basic services to the population through a network of hospitals. Rural health care is provided through Basic Health Units staffed with a health assistant, nurse midwife and a basic health worker.

Since 1961, the health status of the population has remarkably improved with over 90 per cent health coverage with basic services. Over 90 per cent of the population has access to clean drinking water and there is 88 per cent sanitation coverage. There has also been dramatic decrease in mortality and morbidity. As a result, the life expectancy of 33 years in 1960 has risen to 66 today. The population growth rate has decreased from 3.1 per cent in 1994 to 1.8 per cent in 2005. More than 50 per cent of women in labour are attended by trained personnel.

Bhutan leads South Asia in the use of oral Rehydration therapy for preventing deaths from diarrhoea and it was the first country in the regions to iodize its entire salt supply, which has resulted in the virtual elimination of iodine deficiency. Bhutan has achieved universal child immunization and diseases such as polio, neonatal tetanus and diphtheria have been virtually eliminated, while malaria and leprosy are under control today.

Bhutan Health Trust Fund

As Bhutan's development philosophy lays the physical and spiritual well-being of its people within a safe and secure environment, investments in the social sector have always been accorded the highest priority. In the vital sector of health, the key concern of the Government of Bhutan is to enhance the accessibility and quality of primary health care services against rising costs and competing needs. To provide a dependable alternative for financing the priority needs of vaccines, essential drugs and needles and syringes, Bhutan Health Trust Fund (BHTF) was initiated in 1997 by former Health Minister, Lyonpo Sangay Ngedup. The BHTF was formally launched at WHO Headquarters in Geneva on 12 May 1998.

Traditional Medicine Services

Bhutan's traditional medicine services is called *So-Wa-Rigpa* which is based on Indian and Chinese traditions and incorporates ancient medical practices connected with magic and religion. Despite the introduction of modern medicine, *So-Wa-Rig-Pa,* has retained its role in providing health care. Ever since its introduction in the 17th century, So-Wa-Rigpa has played a significant role, along with spiritual remedies offered by religions institutions. It was recognized as the official medical tradition and integrated into the health system in 1967.

Access to traditional medicine in the country has greatly increased with 38 traditional *drungtshos* (doctors) providing traditional medicinal services in all *dzongkhags* of the country.

The rich tradition of indigenous medicine, based primary on herbal treatment is kept alive by the Institute of

Traditional Medicine Services, established in 1998 at Thimphu and 26 traditional Medicine Services, established in 1998 at Thimphu and 26 traditional units scattered across Bhutan. Several forms of treatment are applied in traditional medicine, including indigenous surgical procedures such as *gtar* (blood letting), *bsregs* (cauterization), *gser khap* (acupressure by a golden needle), *tshug* (cauterization with instruments of different herbal compounds), *dugs* (applying heat or cold to parts of the body), *byugspa* (medicated oil massage), *sman-chu* (stone-heated bath), *tsha-chu* (bath at hot spring) and lum (vapour treatment).

Diagnosis is made by the physician mainly through the reading of the pulse. Using the *So-Wa-Rigpa* method, it is possible for physicians to detect diseases of any organ by reading the pulse. The eyes, tongue and urine are also examined for signs which help the diagnosis.

The components of traditional medicine include plants, minerals, animal parts, precious metals and gems which are all used in different combinations to make over three hundred medicines in the form of pills, tablets, powders, ointments and syrups. These traditional medicines are produced entirely for domestic consumption, through there is plan to eventually export them in the future.

TOURISM SERVICE PROVIDERS

Tour Operators

Bhutan has almost 450 Bhutanese tours operators who are the guiding principle of high value low volume and they have common rules and regulation which has been set by the Royal Government of Bhutan. Bhutan Tour Operators provide various types of service to the tourists under the norms and principles of the government.

Association of Bhutan Tour Operators (ABTO)

Association of Bhutan Tour Operators are the association of Bhutanese tour operators come unity to solve problems and raise the issues to the government for the benefit of tourists as well for their sustainability.

Tourism Council of Bhutan (TCB)

Tourism Council of Bhutan is body who has linkage to the government on issues of the tourism. They work on their norms and principle of the tourism. They help the tourism service to run efficiently and effectively.

Hotel Association of Bhutan (HAB)

It is association of the Hoteliers to provide good service to tourists.

Guide Association of Bhutan (GAB)

Guide association of Bhutan is association of tour guides for the effective tour guides and provide good service to tourists.

MEASURING OF DEMAND FORECAST OF TOURISM IN BHUTAN INTERNATIONAL TOURISM

Potential and Current Markets for Bhutan's Tourism Industry

Source Market Summary

United States of America has been the important source market for Bhutan for many years, taking the top position in terms of total arrivals and bed nights. In 2008, there were 6939 tourists from U.S.A. which is a 20.3 per cent increase compared to 2007. It constitute 27.3 per cent of total bed nights fro 2008. Tourists from U.S.A. stay for 8.7 days on an average and 46.8 per cent preferred to visit Bhutan during September, October and November months (Fig. 10.1).

Average Length of Stay

The average length of stay for 2008 was 7.8 days compared to 7.9 days for 2007. The source market with highest average length of stay remained same with visitors

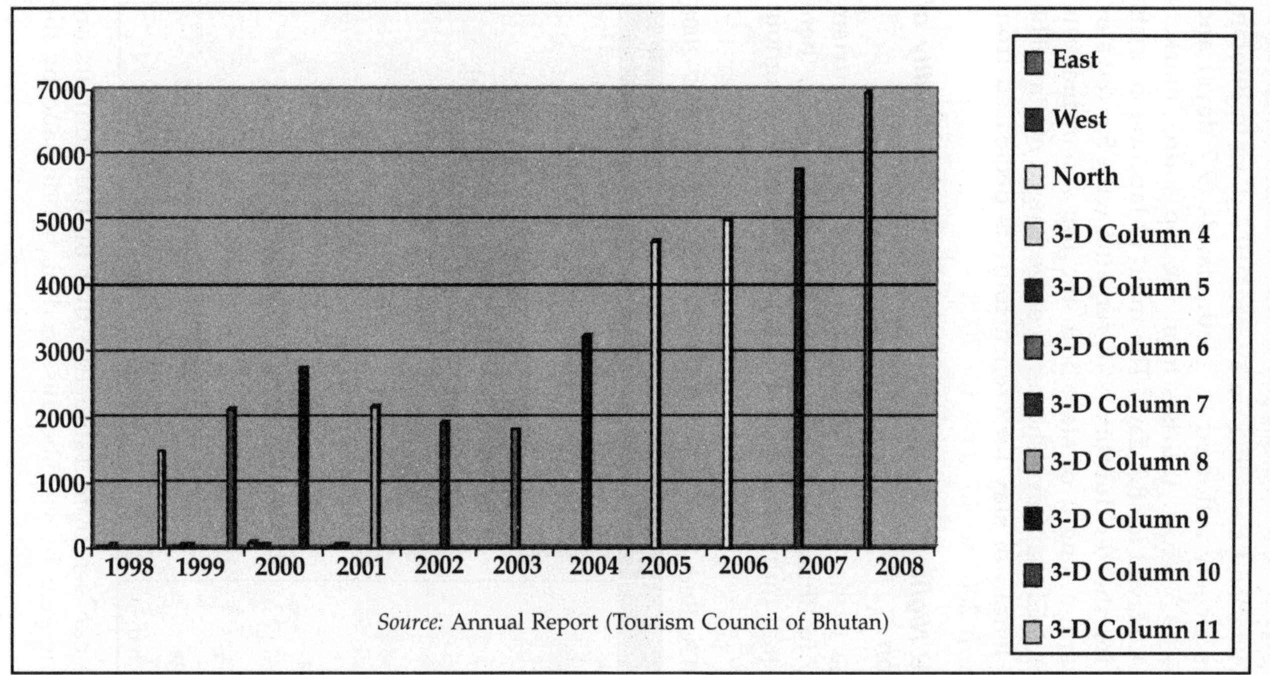

Source: Annual Report (Tourism Council of Bhutan)

Fig. 10.1: Visitor arrival from United States of America.

from Switzerland spending on average 10.4 days in Bhutan. This was closely followed by Netherlands (9.7 days) and Australia (9.5 days). Tourists from the top source market, the U.S.A. stayed for 8.7 days. The trend of Japanese tourists staying for shorter duration still remains with 5.6 days as their average length of stay. Both the top Asian markets (Japan and China) have shorter average length of stay. The average length of stay for French tourists decreased from 9.6 days in 2007 to 8.7 days for 2008.

The Bed Nights Spent by the Tourists of Seasonality of Visitation

One of the major challenges faced by the tourism industry in Bhutan is the seasonality. In other words, there is not equal number of visitors visiting Bhutan throughout the year.

Table 10.3: Bed Nights Spent by the Tourists in 2007-2008

Month	Bed nights 2007	Bed nights 2008	Difference
January	2661	3083	442
February	5838	8659	2821
March	21,246	28,609	7363
April	22,865	24,826	1961
May	7390	12,990	5600
June	4080	6334	2254
July	3384	6776	3392
August	6543	8906	2363
September	24,560	22596	-1964
October	41068	55236	14168
November	22662	34104	11442
December	7617	8064	447

We can see from Table 10.3 that Bhutan tourists are increasing year by year because bed nights demand by the tourists are increasing monthly and yearly. We could see that there is huge difference in demand of bed nights from 2007 to 2008 except September.

Regional Tourism

Source market like India, Bangladesh and Maldives are categories as regional source markets as visitors from these countries do not directly contribute to the government revenue because of the open-border policy. Whereby visitors do not require a visa. Due to this different arrival and visa conditions, these source of markets are not reflected in *tashel* system and have therefore not been included in any of the following tables or graphs. That said, it is not mean that the regional visitors are not important as visitors from India alone outnumber the U.S.A. source market.

In 2007, there were 34,478 Indian tourists who came to Bhutan and out of this 17,344 came solely for holidaying. There was a slight drop in the Indian visitors for 2008 with only 32,285 tourists visiting Bhutan. Out of 32,285 some 52.4 per cent came for holiday purpose.

Demand for Tourism Product in Bhutan by the Different Continents

Europe has demand of 42.32 per cent of Bhutan for visiting, 28.69 per cent by North America, 27.2 per cent by Asia/Asia pacific, 1.12 per cent by North America and .39 per cent by Middle East and .28 per cent by Africa (Table 10.2).

RECOMMENDATIONS

After making a study author has brought down some proposal for further development of industry. Possible ways to improve the industry are listed below.

Further Developing the Tourism Infrastructure

Promoting ecotourism in Bhutan will require the development of appropriate infrastructure. Although this

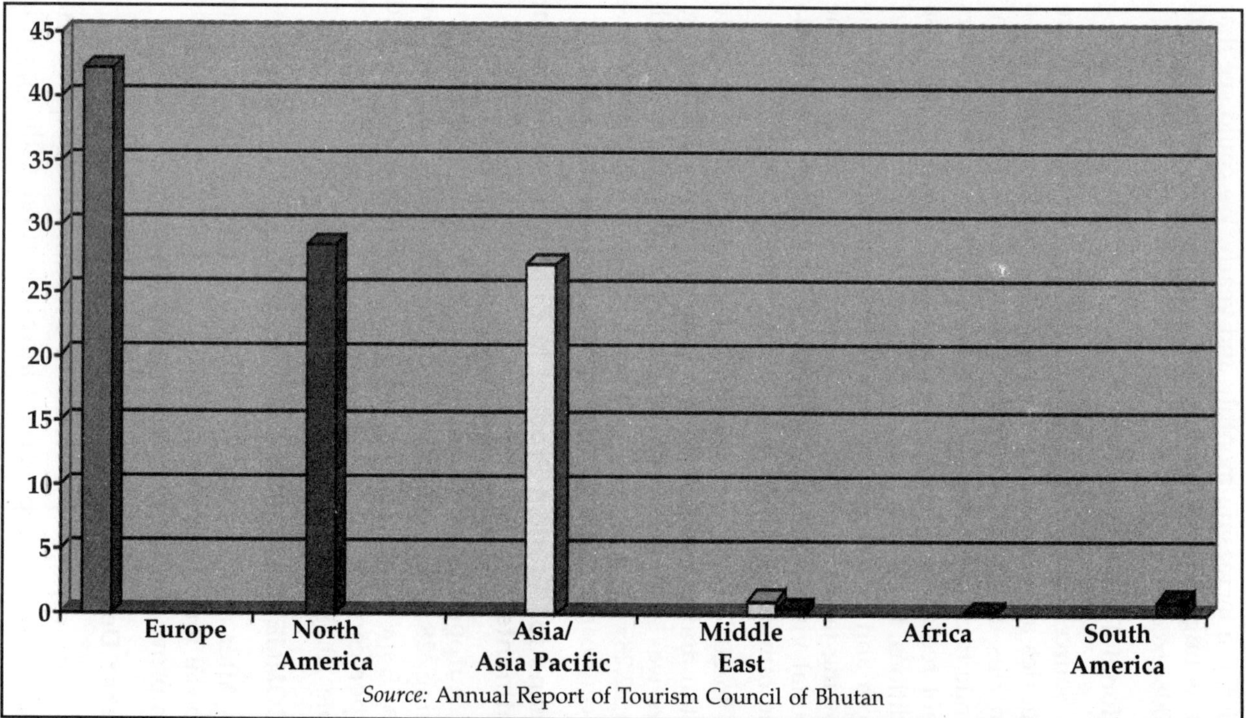

Source: Annual Report of Tourism Council of Bhutan

Fig. 10.2: Demand for Tourism Product in Bhutan by Different Continents.

type of tourism traditionally requires fewer infrastructures than other forms of tourism, many countries have built elaborate facilities within protected areas in the name of ecotourism. Such developments have given ecotourism a bad name with protestors calling it "eco-terrorism" instead. The development of ecotourism in Bhutan should be limited to development of trails and access routes, and basic interpretative facilities like visitor centers. It is recommended that the development of infrastructure for ecotourism in protected areas undergo an Environmental Impact Assessment to ensure the suitability of the project and to prevent costly environmental degradation.

Diversifying the Tourism Products that have a Potential to Attract Tourism to Visit

Tourism in Bhutan is-so-far mostly limited to cultural tourists, sightseers and trekkers. In 2007, out of a total of 21,094 tourists there were 20,191 cultural tourists and 903 trekkers. Although Bhutan has vast potential for other forms of tourism and special interests such as sports tourism, adventure tourism, and nature tourism, the process of product diversification is just beginning. Therefore, diversification of tourism products that has a potential to attract tourism has to be given importance.

Opening Up New Routes within the Country to Spread Out Tourism Benefits

When we contrast the ratio between cultural and trekkers tourists, cultural tourist is far more comparing to trekkers. So, to increase the number of trekker tourists the industry needs to look forward to develop new routes within the country to spread out tourism benefits to country. Not only to open new track routes but also improving the existing track routes is very important to sustain the trekkers group of tourists.

Human Resource Development

The development of human resources, not only within the Department of Tourism, but also within individual private operators and other bodies is a must for the success of future programmes. With careful planning and management of the industry and the appropriate inputs, the tourism industry in Bhutan could well surpass its economic expectations without eroding the cultural and environment of the country. Therefore, the industry needs to look forward to provide training in business development skills and the integration of the principles of social, environmental, corporate responsibility and raise efficiency of the tour operators.

Provide Adequate Training for Guides to Impart Uniform Information to the Clients

A weakness in Bhutan's present tourism is the lack of well-trained and knowledgeable guides, especially for specialist tours like bird watching, photography, and flora tourism. A formal system of training and accreditation will help the country provide the high standards expected by specialist tourists. So, the Department of Tourism needs to conducted several training courses for guides and need to introduce a system of licensing cultural and trekking guides. All guides employed by any tour operator in Bhutan have to be licensed. This ensures that all guides have basic training in trekking and mountaineering techniques and are briefed on all aspects of tourism in Bhutan with special emphasis on the environmental and cultural issues to communicate uniform information to the clients.

Training for Hoteliers to Improve the Hospitably Services

There are no formal hotel and tourism training institutes in the country. Most companies have problems in attracting and keeping adequately trained employees at all levels. As of now there is only few people who are specialize in tourism and hospitality management which leads to lack of manpower at all level. Therefore, the government has to think about establishing the hotel and tourism training institute or sending people to other third countries to get training in tourism and hospitality to improve the hospitality services.

Less Dissemination of Information of Country to Other Third Countries

Although much has been written about Bhutan's rich biodiversity and pristine environment, there is a genuine lack of interpretive materials that can be used by interested visitors to Bhutan and school children, particularly field guides and biodiversity tour guides. For ecotourism to be a success the royal government and the tourism industry needs to invest in the development of basic scientific information on the country's biodiversity.

CONCLUSION

The Royal Government of Bhutan recognizes that tourism is a world-wide phenomenon and an important means of achieving socioeconomic development particularly for a developing country like Bhutan. It also recognizes that tourism, in affording the opportunity to travel, can help in promoting understanding among people and building closer ties of friendship based on appreciation and respect for different cultures and lifestyles. Towards achieving this objective, the Royal Government, since commencement of tourism in the year 1974, has adopted a very cautious approach to growth and development of the tourism industry in Bhutan. In order to minimize the problems, the number of tourists has been maintained at a manageable level and this control on number is exercised through a policy of government regulated tourist tariff "high value low volume".

There are, however, problems associated with tourism which, if not controlled, can have devastating and irreversible impact on the local environment, culture and identity of the people. Realizing these problems and the fact that the resources on which tourism is based are limited, the Royal government of Bhutan recognizes the need to develop the Bhutanese tourism industry based on the principles of sustainability, which means it must be environmentally and economically viable.

REFERENCES

Brandon, Katrin (1996). *Ecotourism and Conservation: A Review of Key Issues,* The World Bank, April, 1996.

Dorji, Tandi, *Sustainability of Tourism,* Communication Officer, National Environment Commission, Thimphu.

Doswell, Roger, The Development of Tourism in Bhutan: A Discussion Paper, World Tourism rganization and the United Nations Development Program, Thimphu.

Economic and Social Commission for Asia and the Pacific (1993). "Management of Sustainable Tourism Development", *ESCAP Tourism Review,* No. 11.

Inskipp, Edward (1992). "Sustainable Tourism Development in the Maldives and Bhutan", *UNEP Industry and Envirnment,* Vol. 15, No. 3-4, July-December 1992.

Ministry of Agriculture (1998). *Biodiversity Action Plan for Bhutan,* Thimphu: Royal Government of Bhutan.

National Environment Commission (1998). "Bhutan: Ecotourism Management Plan for Jigme Dorji National Park" in *The Middle Path: National Environmental Strategy for Bhutan,* Thimphu: Royal Government of Bhutan. Nature Conservation Division, Ministry of Agriculture, Royal Government 1998.

Planning Commission Secretariat (1999). *Bhutan 2020: A Vision for Peace,Prosperity, Happiness,* Thimphu: Royal Government of Bhutan.

USEPA, WWF, UNEP, SEDESOL, VROM (1995). *The Netherlands: Tourism Support Package.*

Customer Relationship Management
A Marketing Tool for Retaining Customers

Rajib Lochan Panigrahy*
Madhusmita Das**

The recent developments in the marketing strategy are the web-based and telephonic techniques with mobile marketing. The companies producing consumer goods and the service providers are doing marketing for their goods or services through websites, mobile telephony with CRM (Customer Relationship Management). They are developing stronger bonds with their customer called as CRM. The CRM is to produce high customer equity. The more loyalty to customer, the more customer equity. It is the customers' tendency to stick with the brand, above and beyond the objective and subjective assessments of its worth. This relationship includes loyalty programme, special recognition and treatment

* Faculty (MBA), Ambedkar College of Management & Technology, Berhampur, (Orissa).

** Faculty (Management Studies), Vignan Institute of Management & Technology, Berhampur, (Orissa).

programmes, community building programs, knowledge building programs. This formulates integrated value management, brand management, relationship management within a customer centric focus. It achieves acquisition, retention of customer and an ad-on selling. It depends on the quality of CRM maintained by the company with the ability to attract, retain talent, customer, investors, partners with relational equity.

CRM is the process of managing detailed information about individual customers and carefully managing the customer service centers or customer touch points to maximize customer loyalty. The customer service centre is a point at which a customer encounter the brand, product and service. It enables companies to provide excellent real time customer service through the effective use of individual account information. To keep customer relationship, to know customer value, companies can customer market offerings, services, programmes, messages and media. CRM is important because a major driver of company's profitability is the aggregate value of the company's customer base.

CRM is a set of strategies, processes, metrics, organizational culture and technology solutions that enhance an organization's ability to see the differences in its customers' and prospects' behaviour and needs, track new opportunities to better serve their customers and act, instantly and profitably, on those differences and opportunities. Recently CRM has taken a center stage in the business world with businesses concentrating on saving money and increasing profits by redefining internal processes and procedures. It costs a company dramatically less to retain and grow an existing client, than it does to court new ones. *"It is seven times more expensive to acquire a new customer than to keep an existing one"*, therefore the value of customer information and management should never be underestimated.

For customer loyalty and equity with company, there are several electronic and mobile techniques formulated in the field of marketing in the name of care concerns, customer care, customer service centres, customer touch points, etc. Contacts, messages, communications, media has played a formidable role in marketing for customer loyalty with the company in the 21st century. There are various technical components of CRM like customer information, sales, marketing trends and marketing efficacy that act in tandem to improve relationship between companies and consumers. From a technological perspective, it involves capturing customer data from across the organization and consolidating all internally and externally acquired customer-related data in a central database. This data is then analyzed and the results of the analysis are distributed via customer touch points like mobile sales force, inbound and outbound call centers, web sites, point-of-sale, email, etc., for use while dealing with customers at these very touch points. The Internet has revolutionized the way business is done and has virtually taken the enterprise information system within the reach of the customer. It can be accessed through the call centers, through the Internet and increasingly through mobile devices. More and more the media and communication, progress with marketing and the organization is progressive. CRM maintains its gravity by mobile telephony and internet services. By mobile telephony and internet infrastructure, customer can easily be communicated messages, services delivery which increases accessibility, maintains and updates real time information. Today mobile telephony became easy to access communication through SMS (Short Mail Service) and pocket internet services in cellular phones made the communication and accessibility easier while moving also. Hence, the trading through mobile called as e-trading or e-business or e-commerce became easier with e-payments through bank called as mobile banking. The recent trend of e-commerce became e-tailing i.e. retailing electronically. With this facility a good CRM technology can maintain customer loyalty for business prospects and retention of customer, trader, partner, talent.

Hence, the CRM is more important to a company for which company should capture customer date, delivering it to customer touch points/service stations for maintaining customer relationship and retention. So, from the customer point of view, well implemented CRM system can offer a "Unified Customer Interface" which means that at each transaction, the relevant account details, knowledge of customer preferences and past transactions, history of a service problem are at a finger tips of the person serving the customer which can result a vast service improvements. So, CRM has a multi dimensional perspective i.e. Customer (buyer) and the firm (seller/service provider) both will get the benefit. From a company perspective, CRM system allow the company to better understand, segment and tier its customers base, better target promotion and cross selling.

A CRM captures all aspects of interaction a company has with its clients. A CRM automates the functions of Sales, Marketing and Support and helps make them efficient and more effective. The CRM is gaining increasing importance in this competitive world. All customers want to be treated individually. On the other hand the organizations want to consolidate all the efforts spent on an account and want to leverage collaborative focus on the customers. Towards this there is a need to maintain all the data relating to accounts, contacts and opportunities as follows:

- Pursue all leads in the best and optimal manner.
- Retrieve all historical data relating to an opportunity – such that bids may be prepared in the most realistic manner.
- Implement organization wide access rights and privileges for the data and information contained in the system.

Paper and Roger outline a four-step framework for one-to-one CRM in marketing as:

1. *Identify your prospects and customers*: Build, maintain and mine a rich customer database with information derived from all the channels and customer touch points essential to identify the ideas for prosperity by identifying the customers.
2. *Differentiate customer:* Treat all customers as most valuable customer. Apply activity based costing, calculate customer life time value with less customer specific servicing costs.
3. *Interact with individual customers* to improve your knowledge about their individual needs and to build stronger relationship.
4. *Customise products, services and messages to each customer,* Facilitate customer-company interaction through the company contact centre and communication media i.e. through email, SMS, websites, prepaid postage letter with envelops, etc.

THE COMMON CRM APPLICATIONS

From the above discussions, CRM requires the following common applications for successful implementation of CRM in a firm having customers:

1. **Data Collection** – the CRM system captures customer data such as personal data, purchase history, consumer preference on willingness and/or ability to purchase, income and family status, livelihood, geographical status, service preference, etc.
2. **Date Analysis** – The collected data are analysed and categorized according to the criteria set by the firm. The customers are to be divided in tier and tailor service to be delivered accordingly.
3. **Sales Force Automation (SFA)** – This system provides an array of capabilities to streamline all phases of the

sales process, minimizing the time that sales representatives need to spend on manual data entry and administration. This allows them to successfully pursue more clients in a shorter amount of time than other possible methods. SFA system is a Contact Management System (CMS) for tracking and recording every stage in the sales process for each prospective client, from initial contact to final disposition. Many SFA applications also include insights into opportunities, territories, sales forecasts and workflow automation, quote generation, and product knowledge. Class sales, after sell service, sells promotion, class sale, sales lead, etc can be tracked and facilitated through CRM system. For pre, during and post sales, CRM is essential. Hence, data analysis determines the nature of customer, customer preference, its cause and affect to retain customer. CRM became a requisite for every business firm to attract, retain and serve customers in the recent age.

4. **Marketing Automation** – Customer data mining enables a firm to target its market. A good CRM system enables a firm to market its product and/or services better to achieve its marketing goal and it will act as a cost saving tool. It results increase in return to investment on its marketing expenditure. A marketing automation helps the enterprise to identify and target its best clients and generate qualified leads for the sales team. A key marketing capability is tracking and measuring multi-channel campaigns, including email, search, social media, and direct mail. Metrics monitored include clicks, responses, leads, deals, and revenue. As marketing departments are increasingly obliged to demonstrate revenue impact, today's systems typically include features for measuring the ROI of campaigns.

5. **Call Centre Automation/Customer Care Service** – Call centres or customer care centres has the personnel set up with telephonic interactions with customers and

interface on internet just at a fingertip which increases customer care services. It is mostly applicable in electronic, media, banking, cellular services. Recognizing that service is an important differentiator, organizations are increasingly turning to technology platforms to help them improve their clients' experience while aiming to increase efficiency and minimize costs. Even so, a 2009 study revealed that only 39 per cent of corporate executives believe their employees have the right tools and authority to solve client problems.". The core for these applications has been and still is comprehensive call center solutions, including such features as intelligent call routing, computer telephone integration (CTI), and escalation capabilities.

RICH MEDIA OF CRM

Internet-based presentation of messages plays an effective role in promoting the image of a company online. Enhancing the earlier modes of audio/video and flash, internet based presentations raise the bar of company-consumer interactivity to a whole new level. The SMS can introduce and maintain relationship of a company with customers which requires a rich database of customers with accurate mobile numbers. Now-a-days the cellular service providers are rendering auto-generated messaging services of a company to their customers or selected customers of the company for advertisement/communication of a company in a very cheap and nominal rate. It is also possible through e-mail. The SMS can also communicate more things to the newly introduced cellular phones where there are 3D facility which can show the MMS (multi media service), internet facility. The mobile users can also open web sites in mobile while they are at off, moving, traveling, sitting/rest time. Technology has been a very rich media of advertisement now-a-days for the benefit of the company and side-by-side it is also beneficiary to the customers to get information need not moving to the shop/out lets/shopping malls/centres.

BENEFITS OF CUSTOMER RELATIONSHIP MANAGEMENT

These tools have been shown to help companies attain these objectives.

- Streamlined sales and marketing processes.
- Higher sales productivity.
- Added cross-selling and up-selling opportunities.
- Improved service, loyalty, and retention
- Increased call center efficiency.
- Higher close rates.
- Better profiling and targeting.
- Reduced expenses.
- Increased market share.
- Higher overall profitability.
- Marginal costing.
- Creates communication.

It has been predicted that the total worldwide market for CRM services will grow to US$ 125.2 billion by 2004. With a vast talent pool India is fast becoming an important development base of major CRM companies. Indian companies and other institutions that offer jobs are jumping into the CRM bandwagon to seize a chunk of the global market, both products as well as services call centres, catering primarily to the American and European markets are coming up in and around the metros. With the easing of infrastructure constraints, India is likely to emerge as a significant player in this segment. India even has a CRM Foundation in New Delhi, founded with the purpose of assessing and improving CRM practices. Although many Indian call centers have come up that cater to international market, there are only a few Indian companies that have actively taken up CRM. The CRM enabled companies include

Tata Telecom, TVS Electronics, HP India, Tata Infotech, Carrier Refrigeration, Tata Teleservices, Satyam Infoway, Planet M, and Epicenter Technologies among many others.

Some of the mobile phone companies in India have started to integrate CRM services to increase the *consumer satisfaction*. For the big mobile operators, customer care is becoming the differentiator. Other sectors like Banking and Insurance services are also deploying CRM solutions. The ICICI Bank and ICICI Prudential Life Insurance along with several other large banking and insurance companies are adopting CRM solutions. Vendors and analysts agree that the need to acquire, retain and support customers will stimulate greater investment in CRM. Like all other IT enabled services, CRM is likely to grow at a rapid pace in India during the next few years.

CHALLENGES OF CUSTOMER RELATIONSHIP MANAGEMENT

Tools and workflows can be complex to implement, especially for large enterprises. Previously these tools were generally limited to contact management, monitoring and recording interactions and communications. Software solutions then expanded to embrace deal tracking, territories, opportunities, and at the sales pipeline itself. Next came the advent of tools for other client-facing business functions. These technologies have been, and still are, offered as on-premises software that companies purchase and run on their own IT infrastructure. Perhaps the most notable trend has been the growth of tools delivered via the Web, also known as cloud computing and software as a service (SaaS). In contrast with traditional on-premises software, cloud-computing applications are sold by subscription, accessed via a secure Internet connection, and displayed on a Web browser. Companies don't incur the initial capital expense of purchasing software; neither must they buy and maintain IT hardware to run it on.

Despite all this, many companies are still not fully leveraging these tools and services to align marketing, sales, and service to best serve the enterprise. Often, implementations are fragmented; isolated initiatives by individual departments to address their own needs. Systems that start disunited usually stay that way: Siloed thinking and decision processes frequently lead to separate and incompatible systems, and dysfunctional processes.

CONCLUSION

With all the discussions above CRM is a tool not only for retaining customers but the stakeholders, traders, partners, well wishers in the trade because all are treated as customers. With the help of all of them, the marketing of an organization can be in growth trend. It requires good database for customers relation to maintain loyalty. The good customer loyalty on trade is a progressive marketing tool which helps the business of the organization towards prosperity. It is only possible with good communication and response towards the customers and it is more simplified with the advancement of technology.

REFERENCES

Lovelock Christopher, Wirtz Jochen, Chatterjee Jayanta, *Service Marketing – People, Technology, Strategy* (2008) 5th Edition, Pearson Education Inc.

Philip, Kotler, Keller Kelvin Lane, Kashy Abraham, Jha Mithileswar, *Marketing Management* (12th Edition), Pearson Education, Prentice Hall Publishers, New Delhi, pp. 127-129.

Index

F

G

H

I

J

K

M

S

T